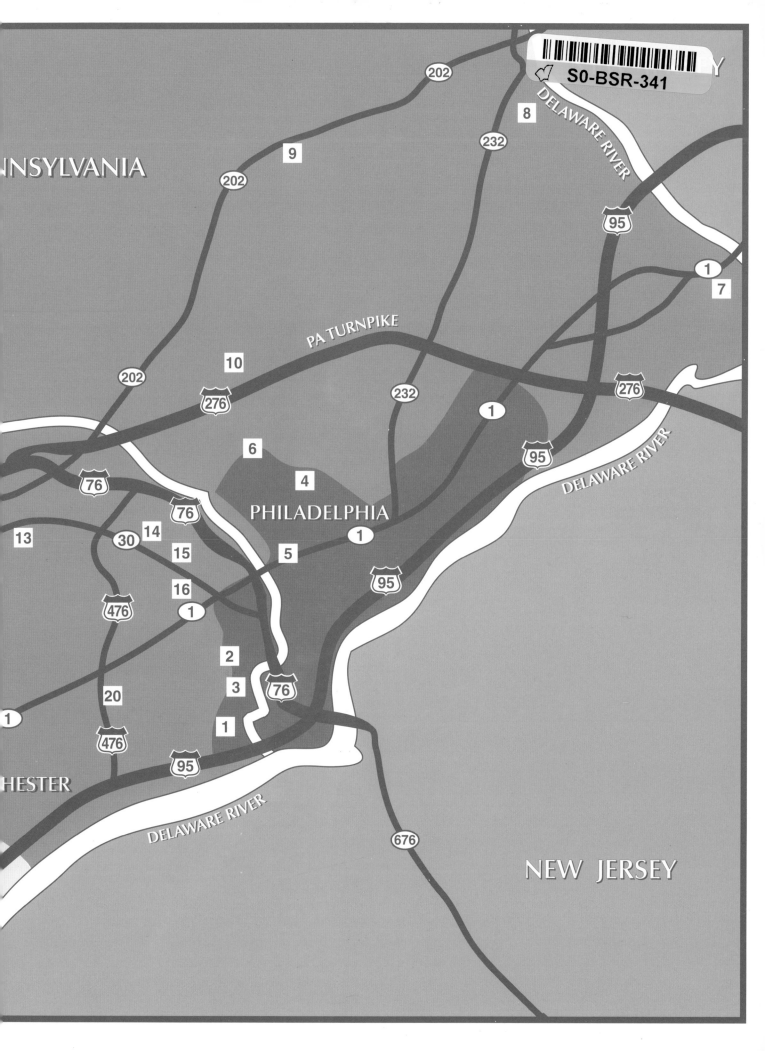

GARDENS OF PHILADELPHIA

GARDENS AND ARBORETUMS
OF THE CITY
AND DELAWARE VALLEY

GARDENS OF PHILADELPHIA
Text © 2004 by John G. Hope
Photographs © 2004 by Blair Seitz
ISBN 1-879441-91-8

Library of Congress Control Number: 2004090128

**RB
BOOKS**
"...richly beautiful"

Seitz and Seitz, Inc.
1010 N. Third Street
Harrisburg, PA 17102
717-232-7944
www.blairseitz.com

Graphic Design by: Meg Ream Design

Printed in Hong Kong

Previous page: *Canna pretoria variegata*,
Longwood Gardens

These pages: *Yarrow achillea spp.* are perennial herbs
displayed in several Philadelphia gardens.

GARDENS OF PHILADELPHIA

BY JOHN G. HOPE
PHOTOGRAPHY BY BLAIR SEITZ

RB
BOOKS
"...richly beautiful"

Harrisburg, PA

Acknowledgements

It's particularly nice when one can do a job that one loves. The three books that Blair Seitz and I have jointly produced—*Westylvania Heritage Trail, Pennsylvania's Scenic Route 6,* and this one—have been labors of love for both of us.

It really can't get any better than to use a beautiful day to walk through one or more garden areas, often in the company of relatives, friends, or pets, being able to take time to stop and drink in the sights, sounds, and smells.

The 20 gardens we feature in this book all have distinct personalities and missions. All are valuable for what they are and what they offer, and all contribute significantly to the quality of life in Philadelphia and its surrounding counties.

Our efforts to bring this book to you were aided by the many staff members and volunteers at each of the venues, who graciously took time to show us around, answered our questions, checked plant identifications, and made sure that we had described their facilities accurately. In some cases, I went to the gardens unannounced, approaching them as just another visitor. I was always struck by the unfailing courtesy and graciousness shown by all those I came across. There must be something about working with plants, flowers, and trees every day, and being continually surrounded by such beauty, that leads people to always be in a good mood when dealing with the public.

Our work in identifying many of the flowers and trees we saw also was made easier by our friend Howard Eyre and his colleagues at Delaware Valley College, who graciously looked at many of the photographs and helped with identification.

Designing a book that features so many beautiful pictures is not easy, and we are grateful to Meg Ream for creating a garden on paper in which to set the many things we saw. Our thanks also to Martha Berg for her thorough and useful index.

And, finally, we express our appreciation to Anna and Ruth for understanding why we were away from our families on so many beautiful days, claiming to be working. There was a lot of effort involved in production of this book, but when you are dealing with so much beauty, it's hard to call it work. ❧

-John G.Hope

Table of Contents

Historic Bartram's Garden

More than 250 years ago, Quaker farmer John Bartram was minding his own business plowing his fields when he saw a daisy, and that chance encounter changed his life. He was so struck by the plant's simplicity and beauty that he and his son William spent much of the rest of their lives exploring, collecting, and trying to understand all forms of nature.

A wonderful place to feel this sense of history and exploration and to understand what Bartram was doing is at the Historic Bartram's Garden, the southwest Philadelphia home and garden of America's pioneering family of naturalists, botanists, and explorers.

Born outside of Philadelphia to a Quaker family in Darby Township, Bartram did not have a formal education, but taught himself through observation, reading, and correspondence with equally inquiring minds in the colonies and abroad.

From his 102-acre farm in Philadelphia, which he bought in 1728, Bartram traveled north to Lake Ontario, south to Florida, and west to the Ohio River in search of plants and natural history specimens for his own botanic garden and for collectors at home and abroad. He and William are credited with identifying and introducing into cultivation more than 200 of our native plants.

Today, Historic Bartram's Garden is a fascinating study in contrasts. It lies near the intense noise and bustle of Philadelphia International Airport and in the shadow of One Liberty Place and the other tall buildings that grace the Philadelphia skyline. At the river's edge in the garden, you can look across to the active oil refineries with their storage tanks and fires that light the sky.

But in the garden you have a sense of peace and calm as well as awe at the thought that George Washington, Benjamin Franklin, Thomas Jefferson and many others were all present where you are now standing.

One of my aunts, Gertrude Laing, remembered hearing of some type of connection between the Bartrams and our family, but didn't know any of the details. While I couldn't find evidence of any relationship in the books at the Garden's gift shop, I was very interested to see a reference to a Dr. John Hope, who was a professor of botany and medicine at the University of Edinburgh in Scotland and contacted Bartram to order plants to be shipped to him there. Hope formed a group, which came to be known as the Society of Gentlemen, to continue to import seeds and plants for a botanic garden in Scotland. Over time, the group became so impressed with Bartram that it awarded him a gold medal, which was entrusted to Benjamin Franklin to deliver.

After my visit to the garden, I learned from my uncle Thomas Hope, Gertrude's youngest

The American Yellowwood **(LEFT)**, *Cladrastis kentuckea*, was discovered on limestone cliffs in Kentucky and Tennessee and now is planted as far north as Boston. Leaves are described as silver velvet in spring and turn clear yellow in fall. Fragrant white flowers of a large sweet pea type sprout from the ends of twigs in early summer, bending them over with their weight so that clusters dangle like wisteria and the tree is visited by many bees.

Carolina Silverbell **(RIGHT)**, *Halesia tetraptera*, is a short-lived, small tree that produces white, bell-shaped flowers in mid-spring. The soft wood is used for pulpwood, cabinets and woodenware.

brother, that my great-great-grandmother had a sister who had married a John Bartram who was descended from the famous Bartram family. In fact, at one time in our family there was a cut glass cake plate that had belonged to the Bartrams. Since it was from my paternal grandmother's side of the family, the name wasn't Hope and that's why I hadn't seen any reference to the Hopes. It really can be a very small world with not much separation between people and families.

The grounds include a common flower garden and a riverside meadow and river trail. Near the river is a cider press carved from bedrock. There are specimens of the *franklinia allatamaha* that the Bartrams saved from extinction and named for John Bartram's good friend Benjamin Franklin. Also there is the oldest gingko tree in the country.

Tours of the Bartram house are offered for a fee several times a day and it's worth seeing

Smooth Blackhaw **(ABOVE)**, *Vibernum prunifolium*, occurs as a small, bushy tree or large shrub. It has alligator-hide patterned bark, just as the flowering dogwood does, but its bark is corkier than that of the dogwood. The flowers occur in upright, flat-topped clusters of small, white flowers, making it a popular ornamental.

Spring Beauty **(RIGHT)**, *Claytonia virginica*, was named in honor of John Clayton, one of the earliest Virginia botanists. In early spring the star-like white-to-rose flowers of spring beauty carpet many moist, rich woodlands and sunny stream banks.

for the additional information about this remarkable family provided by the guides. On the day my brother Warren and I were there, we were joined for the tour by two couples, one of whom said they had played in the gardens many years before and could remember when the house tour cost 25 cents instead of the current $5. "John (Bartram) was a friend of ours; it seems that long ago," the man joked.

The house contains period furnishings and artifacts as well as scientific instruments Bartram used. We learned that by 1765, John Bartram's international reputation had earned him the notice of King George III, who honored him as Royal Botanist, a position he held until his death in 1777.

William Bartram identified 213 North American bird species and tracked avian migration paths. He also created the first American bird migration calendar and kept detailed

Oriental Poppy **(BELOW)**, *Popaver orientale*, with its huge, bowl-shaped blossoms, is native to the southern Mediterranean region. Historians tell us the cultivation of poppies dates back to the remotest antiquity.

Ginkgo **(RIGHT)**, *Ginkgo biloba*, has played a crucial role in Chinese herbal medicine for many centuries. Only recently has western medicine begun to seriously study the medicinal uses of ginkgo and realize that it might help treat Alzheimer's disease and increase circulation.

meteorological observations. William Bartram mentored Alexander Wilson, who was John James Audubon's predecessor in bird illustration, introducing him to leading natural history figures in Philadelphia and inspiring him to study birds.

In 1783, the Bartrams issued the first printed plant catalog in America and supplied plants for Independence Hall, Mount Vernon, and Monticello. John Bartram's granddaughter, Ann Bartram Carr, and her husband Robert continued the family tradition in the first half of the 19th century, preserving the Bartram botanic garden and establishing a commercial nursery.

In 1850 Philadelphia industrialist Andrew Eastwick purchased the property and built a home on a hill near the garden "so that not a bush of this beloved old garden shall be disturbed. My dearest hope is that the garden shall be preserved forever."

Blue False Indigo **(RIGHT)**, *Baptisia australis*, rivals the lupine for beauty and structure, but is easier to grow. Wild indigo is an ornamental member of the pea family, with blue-green foliage, topped by magnificent stalks of flowers in early spring.

Redbud **(BELOW)**, *Cercis Canadensis*, is the only wild American tree with bright purple-red flowers. Flowers cover the tree, springing out from twigs, main branches, and even the trunk. The leaves are round hearts. This specimen stands guard at Bartram Gardens over a magnificent view of downtown Philadelphia.

Hackberry **(FAR RIGHT)**, *Celtis occidentalis*, is often mistaken for an elm tree. The tree produces berries the size of peas dangling singly along a twig. When ripe, they are dark purple and sweet to eat.

In 1891, city councilman Thomas Meehan, who was Eastwick's gardener 40 years earlier, succeeded in persuading the city government to acquire Bartram's Garden as a public park. Preservation today includes conservation of the Bartram house and outbuildings, restoration of the wildflower meadow and water garden, construction of a tidal wetland along the Schuylkill River, and enrichment of the historic garden with native plants of the Bartram period.

Visitors Information

Grounds open dawn to dusk all year. House tours and museum shop open Wednesdays to Sundays, 12 noon to 4 p.m., May to October; Wednesdays to Fridays, 12 noon to 4 p.m., November to April. Admission fee for house tour; grounds free.

Historic Bartram's Garden
54th Street and Lindbergh Boulevard • Philadelphia, PA 19143
(215) 729-5281 • http://www.bartramsgarden.org

Japanese House and Garden

Tucked away in a corner of Philadelphia's Fairmount Park near the Horticulture Center is Pine Breeze Villa or Shofuso, the Japanese House and Garden, one of the most unusual attractions in a unique city.

The building was originally built for display in the courtyard of New York's Museum of Modern Art in 1954-55 to show U.S. citizens the essence of Japanese architecture. It was designed by Junzo Yoshimura, who knew Japanese traditional buildings and led Japanese modern architecture with his beautiful designs and imaginative details. The house was built after Shoin-zukuri (desk-centered), a 16th century house style. While at first glance it looks like simply a copy of the model that was used, Kojo-in, in reality there is much of Yoshimura's originality in it.

He changed the plan to enhance the spatial relationship between the garden and the building and to facilitate visitors' movement through the exhibit. He added a teahouse, a kitchen, and a bath to make the house seem functional and to illustrate the Japanese way of life. The Museum of Modern Art exhibition drew three times as many people as had been expected.

Philadelphia's Fairmount Park is no stranger to Japanese architecture. At the U.S. centennial exhibition in the park in 1876, a Japanese townhouse was built by Japanese carpenters and drew much attention. Later, where Shofuso now stands, there was a Japanese temple gate built in the early 1500s and brought to the U.S. for the 1904 St. Louis exposition. It had been purchased by two Philadelphians who appreciated its beauty, but was destroyed by fire in 1955.

The site of the Japanese House and Garden in Philadelphia's West Fairmount Park was first landscaped in Japanese style for the Centennial Exposition of 1876. The garden shown here, now maintained by the Friends of the Japanese House and Garden, was designed by Sano Tansai in 1958, when the house was moved to Philadelphia from the Museum of Modern Art in New York City.

For the Bicentennial Celebration of 1976, the garden was extensively renovated by Nakajima Kenji, to make it one of America's finest and most authentic gardens in the Momoyama style of early 17th century Japan.

Horticultural Center, Fairmont Park

After the Museum of Modern Art exhibition ended, the Japanese House was moved to its location in Fairmount Park where, with the Japanese Garden, it now welcomes more than 10,000 visitors a year.

Be sure to wear socks when you visit the Japanese House. As is the custom in Japan, you will be asked to remove your shoes and leave them in a rack at the entrance to the house before walking around its perimeter and in some of the rooms. (Paper slippers are available for those who don't have socks on.)

The house is striking in its simplicity and peacefulness. The main room is focused on the desk built into one wall and used while sitting on the floor. You can imagine yourself writing letters to friends while sitting at the desk in such calm and beautiful surroundings. In Japan, the house would have been appropriate for an educated member of the upper class, such as a government official, high-ranking priest, or wealthy scholar.

A self-guiding tour with an informative book lent to those who visit winds around the main rooms and then into the kitchen and bath. Visitors then reclaim their shoes and go on into the garden, using stepping-stones on the main path.

The garden was designed by Sano Tansai to incorporate existing landscape elements into a garden that was styled after the 16th and 17th centuries. The area is bordered by a high wall topped with ceramic tiles.

A wooden gate opens into a formal walkway that leads to the main entrance to the house. Within the garden there are stone and wooden bridges, a stone pagoda donated by the city of Kyoto, and a life-size statue of Jizo, a Buddhist deity associated with the salvation of small children.

Some 250 of the rocks decorating the garden were imported from Japan with the house in 1954. In the pond are many large koi, Japanese carp that are trained to come to the house for feeding.

Traditional plants of Japan such as bamboo, pine, hinoki cypress, flowering plum, and azaleas are propagated in harmony with local species. The garden is laid out to give an illusion of depth and size greater than it is, and the rocks, pond, and trees recall the mountains, streams, and forests of Japan.

Outside, there are large Fairmount Park signs that go into great detail about what activities visitors may not engage in. But inside, there is an air of beauty, peacefulness, and calm that quiets one and encourages reflection and meditation.

Note: Visiting hours at the Japanese House may differ from what appears on some printed materials. Also, the Japanese House Web site is **not** http://www.shofuso.org as shown on some brochures. In fact, that is a portal to a number of adult Web sites. To learn more about the house and garden, be sure to go to http://www.shofuso.com.

Visitors Information
Open Tuesdays to Sundays, May 1 to Labor Day, 10 a.m. to 4 p.m; Saturdays and Sundays, 10 a.m. to 4 p.m., September and October. Closed November to April. Admission fee. Group tours by reservation.

Japanese House and Garden
West Fairmount Park • North Horticultural Drive at Montgomery Drive • Philadelphia, PA 19131 (215) 729-5281 • http://www.shofuso.com

Sawara False Cyprus **(RIGHT)**, *Chamaecyparis pisifera 'Filifera Aurea'*, has threadlike branch tips that weep gracefully and bear small cones at maturity. This tree rests on the roof of the Japanese House in Philadelphia's Fairmount Park.

WalKing through the garden **(FAR RIGHT)** at the Japanese House brings visitors a sense of peace and calm.

Tulip, **(NEXT PAGES)**, *Tulipia*, is probably one of the first flowers cultivated for its beauty, as witness this scene at the Fairmount Park Horticultural Center near the Japanese House. Tulip designs have been found on pottery jars dated from 200 to 1600 BC, and tulips were found on the border of a 9th century Byzantine fabric. Tulips were first brought to America by Dutch colonists who settled in the northeast. A stylized tulip with three petals is a dominant feature in Pennsylvania Dutch folk art. It is referred to as the Trinity Tulip, and symbolizes the Trinity as well as faith, hope and charity.

Garden

I grew up in Philadelphia, a city rich in places for children to explore, and one of our favorites was always the Philadelphia Zoo, especially when my Aunt Gina was working at one of the concession stands and there might be an opportunity for some extra candy or food. There were school trips to the Zoo as well as family outings. I made sure to take my own children there to see the many improvements and expansions that have taken place over the years, and now can look forward to showing grandchildren around America's first zoo.

When I was growing up, the official name for the facility was the Philadelphia Zoological Garden and it's easy to understand why when you realize that it is not only home to more than 1,600 rare and exotic animals from around the world, but that it sits on 42 acres of picturesque gardens. The varied collection includes more than 2,400 trees, 5,500 shrubs, 6,500 perennials, and grasses, vines, and ferns.

(LEFT) From 400 feet in the air, visitors using the Philadelphia Zoo Balloon get a bird's-eye view of the nation's oldest zoo, including baskets of petunias seen here through a metal arbor.

River Birch **(BELOW)**, *Betula nigra*, also known as red birch, is often used as an ornamental in landscape plantings because of its showy bark that can range from a silvery gray to reddish brown. This tree overlooks the hippo pool at the Philadelphia Zoo, under the watchful gaze of a marble lion.

But it is the animals that are the stars of the show. Visitors can see the primate reserve with orangutans, lowland gorillas, lemurs, langurs, and gibbons; a rare animal conservation center; a reptile and amphibian house; the first giant otters exhibited in the U.S.; the Treehouse activity discovery center; and the world's first children's zoo, with a petting yard and live animal shows.

Visitor Information
Open daily, except June 14, December 24, 25, and 31, and January 1, with hours varying by the season. Admission fee.

Philadelphia Zoo
3400 W. Girard Avenue • Philadelphia, PA 19104
(215) 243-1100 • http://www.phillyzoo.org

Flowering Dogwood **(BELOW)**, *Cornus florida*, is America's most decorative tree, holding the same kind of reputation among trees that the robin has among birds. All the flowers on the tree unroll at the same time and are extended in layers with shadowy spaces between the blossoms that accentuate the effect. Here a dogwood in full flower frames the entrance to the Philadelphia Zoo's Tortoise Trail.

Crabapple **(RIGHT, TOP)**, *Malus coronaria*, are beautiful in bloom, as attested by this specimen, but are equally attractive in autumn when they produce brightly colored ornamental fruits, often edible. A wild apple species that is a parent of cultivated garden apples, they make a delicious jelly.

Visitors riding in the Philadelphia Zoo's hot air ballon **(RIGHT, BOTTOM)** are treated to a show of spring floral beauty.

Doublefile Viburnum **(RIGHT)**, *Viburnum plicatum tomentosum*, originally was found in China and Japan. In the spring it produces masses of white, sometimes pink, flowers along horizontal branches.

Sycamore **(BELOW)**, *Platanus occidentalis*, contends with tulip tree for the title as biggest tree in the American woods.

Locust **(FAR RIGHT)**, *Robinia*, was named to honor Jean Robin (1550-1629), herbalist to the king of France. In the eastern United States, where it is native, it grows from 70 to 80 feet high with a trunk three or four feet in diameter. It is one of the most valuable timber trees of the American forest.

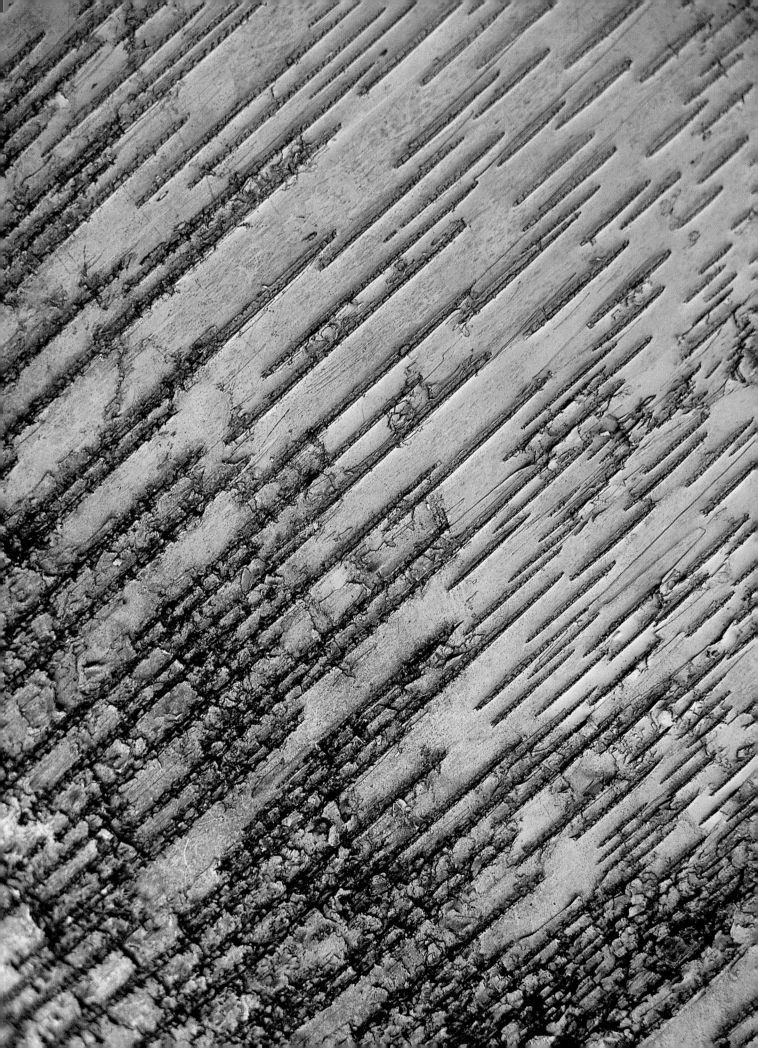

Awbury Arboretum

Located in Philadelphia's busy East Germantown neighborhood, Awbury originally was the summer home of the family of Quaker shipping merchant Henry Cope, who purchased the property in 1852 and named it Awbury after the village of Avebury in England from which his family originally emigrated. Awbury soon became a year-round home for members of the extended Cope family.

Various Victorian and Colonial Revival houses were built between 1860 and the 1920s, forming what is described as a unique cultural landscape. Except for the Francis Cope House, built in 1860, which now is the arboretum headquarters, all of the houses are now privately owned.

Awbury's grounds were laid out in the 19th century in the English landscape garden tradition with the advice of celebrated horticulturalist William Saunders, who designed the National Cemetery at Gettysburg and the Capitol grounds in Washington, D.C. In Saunders' design, long vistas are framed by clusters of trees and shrubs that are interwoven with open space, creating a sharp visual contrast.

At the 2002 annual meeting of the Awbury Arboretum Association, garden historian Elizabeth McLean talked about the Quaker commitment to gardens evident in the work of the Copes and Saunders. "There was not a Quaker style," she said, "but rather an attitude toward landscape, which was similar to their attitude towards life. It reflected an appreciation of nature, and a desire for simplicity—that things be 'plain but handsome' and how simplicity was defined was very much a personal choice."

Concern for preservation of this open space in the heart of the city led members of the Cope family to establish the arboretum in 1916. It is now a non-profit association with a mission to "preserve and interpret Awbury's historic house and landscape, thereby connecting an urban community with nature and history."

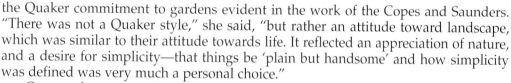

Paper Birch **(LEFT)**, *Betula papyrifera*, has bark that peels off in paper strips, giving it the scientific name *papyrifera*, which means "paper bearing." The paper birch grows from a seed carried by the wind. Although officially known as the paper birch, this tree is also called the white birch and the canoe birch. Indians made their canoes and coverings for their houses with its bark.

The Francis Cope House **(ABOVE)**, a Gothic stone mansion, is the Visitor Center for Awbury Arboretum, one of the last remaining Victorian country estates, and is surrounded by 55 acres of meadows, woodlands, ponds, and gardens.

The Awbury Association has been working hard to preserve the property's woody tree collection and open new garden areas. It has an active nature program for children and other outreach efforts.

On the porch of the Cope House, pick up a Visitor Map that provides interesting information about the many stops on your walking tour.

<u>**Visitors Information**</u>
Open daily dawn to dusk. Free admission.

The Francis Cope House
One Awbury Road • Philadelphia, PA 19138 • (215) 849-5561 • http://www.awbury.org

Golden Raintree **(BELOW)**, *Koelreuteria paniculata*, can draw attention all summer with its beautiful dark green foliage, foot-long golden cascades of flowers in July, and bright green seed pods that turn to beige and last throughout the winter. Flowers dry into interestingly-shaped "pods" that resemble Japanese lanterns. It is one of the few yellow flowering trees.

American Basswood **(RIGHT)**, *Tilia americana*, also known as American linden, is native to all of New England and the Midwestern United States. American basswood is a favorite tree of bees as they extract nectar from its flowers, making a very high-quality honey in the process. The weak wood of this tree is both lightweight and odorless, making it the wood of choice for packing food into boxes and crates.

Sweet Birch **(BELOW)**, *Betula lenta*, has bark and leaves that are sweet and aromatic. The bark, which contains a volatile oil similar to wintergreen oil, is used for medicinal and flavoring purposes.

Wyck

Wyck was home to nine generations of the same Quaker family, the Wistars and the Haines, who owned and lived on this farm in the Germantown section of Philadelphia. Today the colonial house with its 1824 alterations by William Strickland and historic gardens invites visitors to view remarkable collections and to experience the changing character of the city as seen through the eyes and experiences of its owners.

Wyck's earliest owner was Hans Milan, a Quaker who came from Germany and was a descendant of a Swiss Mennonite family. His daughter Margaret married a Dutch Quaker named Dirk Jansen, a linen weaver who prospered in the first half of the 18th century. Their daughter Catherine married Caspar Wistar, a German who became a Quaker and amassed a sizeable fortune as a button maker, glassmaker, and land investor. Ownership of the property continued through several other generations until in the eighth generation, Jane B. Haines founded the first school for horticulture for women, the Pennsylvania School of Horticulture of Ambler, which is now Temple University's Ambler campus. The last owners, Robert and Mary Haines, were fruit growers. Robert patented a device to press apples for a more natural tasting juice.

Wyck is described as an architecturally innovative house with an old-fashioned skin. From the outside it appears colonial in plan and design with some fashionable accents such as 18th century whitewashed stucco.

The house actually is a collection of 18th century parts—the hall (1700-1720), the front parlor (1736), and the library and dining room (1771-1773), which replaced a 1690 log structure.

The house has not been changed significantly since 1824 when Philadelphia architect William Strickland dramatically rearranged its interior spaces to create an open plan, allowing light to flood each room and bringing the pleasures of the garden inside.

Roses climb the walls of Wyck, which was home to nine generations of the same Quaker family, the Wistars and the Haines, who owned and lived on this "farm" in Philadelphia's Germantown section. The grounds include a nationally known garden of old roses (more than 30 varieties) that grow in their original plan dating from the 1820s. Seen here is Rosa 'tausendshin' Rambler.

When purchased in 1689, the property contained about 50 acres. Over the generations, it changed from farmland to a gentleman's summer retreat to a home where Reuben Haines III could pursue scientific agriculture.

The family sold off parcels of land in the 1850s when Germantown was becoming the most desirable of Philadelphia's Victorian-era suburbs.

Today, Wyck's two acres include Jane's rose garden, which grows in its original plan from the 1820s, the park-like lawn with flower borders and spring bulbs, the herb and vegetable gardens, and the original outbuildings from the late 18th and early 19th centuries—the coach house, the ice house, and the smoke house.

White rose of York **(RIGHT)**, *Rosa 'semi-plena'*, climbs a fence at Wyck. **BELOW**, *Peegee Hydrangea, Hydrangea paniculata grandiflora*, will grow and bloom in a wide variety of climates. The name paniculata comes from the fact that the blooms are somewhat panicle-shaped (cone-shaped) rather than ball-shaped.

The white-bloomed flower climbing the fence **(FAR RIGHT)** is Pearlbush, *Exocorda racemosa*, whose buds resemble pearls.

An historical marker at the site says it was used as a British field hospital during the Battle of Germantown on October 4, 1777.

Visitors Information
Open Tuesdays and Thursdays 12 noon to 4:30p.m., and Saturdays, 1p.m. to 4 p.m., April 1 to December 15, and by appointment at other times. Admission fee.

Wyck
6026 Germantown Avenue • Philadelphia, PA 19144
(215) 848-1690 • http://www.wyck.org

Morris Arboretum

All of the gardens in this tour are wonderful sites that have unique things to recommend them. But sometimes you hit something that seems absolutely perfect, and that was my experience at Morris. I don't know if it was the weather, my own mood, the location, or what, but I came away wishing I lived close enough to become a member of the Morris Arboretum and visit it regularly.

The arboretum has been designated as the official arboretum of the Commonwealth of Pennsylvania and its association with the University of Pennsylvania seems evident in the educational approach that is taken and the funding and expertise available to support it.

The property in 1887 was known as Compton, the summer home of brother and sister John and Lydia Morris. The family got its money from the I.P. Morris Company, an iron manufacturing firm founded by their father and later run by John Morris.

When the Morrises purchased their land in Philadelphia's Chestnut Hill section, it was barren, with poor soil that drained too quickly. But with diligent care they surrounded their home with a landscape and plant collection devoted to beauty and knowledge.

John Morris was a noted plantsman and community leader who explored the new world of knowledge available to Victorians. He and his sister traveled widely in America, Asia, and Europe, bringing ideas, artwork, crafts, and plants back to Compton. They shared a love of history and art, and established a tradition of placing sculpture in the garden that continues today.

John and Lydia Morris, who wanted to be judged worthy stewards of their property, laid plans for a school and laboratory at Compton devoted to horticulture and botany. Through the stewardship and vision of that Quaker family, Compton became the Morris Arboretum of the University of Pennsylvania in 1932. It is listed on the National Register of Historic Places and is today an interdisciplinary center that

Peony **(ABOVE)**, *paeonia cv.*, is a single white cultivar. Peonies are a widely distributed group of plants occurring primarily in mountainous regions throughout central and southern Europe, China, Japan, and the northwestern United States. They have a rich association with human culture throughout China where they have long been valued as both medicinal and ornamental plants.

White Ash **(LEFT)**, *Fraxinus americana*, is the most abundant of the ash trees, which play an active role in our lives through tennis rackets, baseball bats, snowshoes, bushel baskets, butter tubs, and oars.

integrates art, science, and the humanities. Thousands of rare and lovely woody plants, including many of Philadelphia's oldest, rarest, and largest trees, are set in a romantic 92-acre Victorian landscape garden of winding paths, streams, flowers, and special garden areas.

One of the most outstanding features of the estate is the collection of large and stately trees placed throughout the property. Beginning with John Morris' interest in growing plants from around the world, unusual specimens have flourished on the site of the Morris Arboretum for more than 100 years. Morris director of horticulture Anthony Aiello says that the staff today continues the Morrises' legacy "by caring for our mature trees and continuing to expand our tree collection."

Maybe the attraction I felt for Morris the day I was there comes from this philosophy printed in one of its attractive brochures: "Please walk on our grass, sit

Phlox **(LEFT, TOP LEFT BACKGROUND)**, *Phlox paniculata 'Robert Poore'*, is a garden phlox cultivar that typically grows in an upright clump three to four feet tall. Spike Speedwell **(FOREGROUND)**, *Veronica spicata 'Royal Candles'*, is a relatively new variety that starts blooming in late spring and early summer.

Rocket Larkspur **(LEFT, TOP RIGHT, TOP OF FRAME)**, *Consolida ambigua*, also is known as annual delphinium. These natives of southern Europe are easy to grow and quickly form tall flower spikes. Below the larkspur is Cranesbill Geranium, *Geranium sanguineum*.

Evergreen Candytuft **(WHITE BLOOMS AT LEFT, BOTTOM)**, *Iberis sempervirens*, gets its scientific name from Iberia, the ancient name for Spain, where several species of this plant grow wild. The "candy" in candytuft is from Candia, the ancient name of Crete.

Purple Rock Cress **(PURPLE BLOOMS AT LEFT, BOTTOM)**, *Aubrieta deltoidea*, is a low-growing, ground-covering plant that produces mauve-purple flowers.

Primrose **(ABOVE)**, *Primula sp.*, has a variety of colorful blooms.

Champlain Rose **(RIGHT)**, *Rosa 'Champlain'*, shown in the rose garden, was developed in Canada for cold hardiness.

under our trees, listen to the birds and fountains, rest and refresh your soul. There's always something to enjoy at Morris Arboretum and Gardens."

Use the Visitor Map you receive when you drive through the entrance station to plan your walk through the gardens. Or, better yet, just walk and discover the pleasures that await you no matter which way you go.

More than 13,000 labeled plants are grown at Morris, including representatives of the temperate flowers of North America, Asia, Africa, and Europe, with a focus on Asian temperate species. Plants collected in China by E.H. Wilson in the early 1900s are the foundation of the historic Asian collection. In addition, many of the Delaware Valley's trees of record (largest of their kind) are found at Morris. Significant plant groups in the collections include maples, magnolia species, native azaleas, members of the witchhazel family, roses, hollies, and conifers. The diversity of the collection means there is something of interest no matter what season you visit the arboretum.

Wherever you look, it seems, your eye falls on something interesting, unusual, or beautiful. As I headed down one path, I turned to see the Green Man, a sculpture carved in the summer of 2002 from the trunk of a 100-year-old European beech.

One of the things I appreciate most about Morris is the extensive information available at various sites throughout the property. Trees and plants aren't just labeled with scientific and popular names as at most gardens. Also included are interesting facts, folklore, scientific data, and other things to provide a context and interest to what is seen.

I learned that the Green Man is an ancient archetype that occurs in art and architecture throughout Europe. It represents the spirit of the woods and vegetation, and signifies irrepressible life, the power of revival, and rejuvenation. Presence of this sculpture on the grounds symbolizes the arboretum's purpose in protecting and

Dwarf Alberta Spruce **(ABOVE, FOREGROUND)**, *Picea glauca 'Conica'*, is a miniature, cone-shaped tree that grows very slowly (2 to 4 inches per year) and rarely needs pruning. Its dense, bright green foliage makes it attractive. It is primarily a novelty specimen plant and is often used as a container plant. Spruces such as this are excellent outdoor bonsai for beginners. Dwarf Twisted Hinoki (False Cypress) **(ABOVE)**, *Chamaecyparis obtusa*, has a moderate growth rate and does not appreciate air pollution.

The Morris Arboretum is particularly good for the information it provides visitors who walk the grounds. Here **(RIGHT)** a sign tells about the medicinal uses of many plants that have been gathered together at the arboretum.

nurturing plants, landscapes, and natural environments and is dedicated to the arboretum's horticulture staff.

Not too far from the administration building is the Garden Railway with its scale model buildings and landscape scenes from the Delaware Valley and G-scale (1/29) model trains that run during the summer and early fall months.

Garden railways date back to the 19th century when railroading was popular in Europe. Scale models of potential projects were built to entice investors and test track layouts. Such garden railways were all the rage in this country before World War II but then died out, until all-weather electric trains sparked new interest in the 1970s. Today it is estimated that 3,800 U.S. gardens have a railway running in them.

Walking across the grass I came unexpectedly across a Madeleine Butcher sculpture of Saint Francis of Assisi, the patron saint of ecologists. She has created him with his head tilted up as if to greet the birds that fly through the area. The sculpture is off the path in a meadow, meaning that you have to be willing to leave the established areas to find and appreciate it.

Nearby is Buky Schwartz' Inside Out. Schwartz took a limestone slab and sliced it into four sections and then worked the interior of each section until it was smooth. The four sections were arranged inside out, drawing visitors to walk into the sculpture to explore the raw outer surfaces.

Along another walk I discovered the Overlook Garden that combines an English rock garden with a Japanese garden, climbing up a small hill toward a busy street outside the property.

As I sat on a bench near the Overlook Garden, I wrote in my notebook that Morris Arboretum is not a garden to be rushed through. It deserves to be visited often and lovingly appreciated because there will always be something new to discover.

Visitors Information
Open daily 10 a.m. to 4 p.m. except Thanksgiving, December 24, 25, and 31, and New Year's Day. Guided public tours year-round on Saturdays and Sundays at 2 p.m. Other tours by reservation. Admission fee.

Morris Arboretum of the University of Pennsylvania
100 Northwestern Avenue • Philadelphia, PA 19118
(215) 247-5777 • http://www.morrisarboretum.org

(LEFT) There are many striking works of sculpture throughout the arboretum grounds, including B.K.S. Iyengar, a dynamic geometric by Robert M. Engman.

Coneflower **(LEFT, BOTTOM)**, *Echinacea purpurea*, works well in cut flower arrangements. "Echinacea" is from the Greek word for hedgehog and refers to the mass of prickly spines that are on the flower's seed head. At one time, it was used extensively in this country as medicine for ailments such as colds, snakebite, and scurvy.

Fountain Grass **(BELOW)**, *Pennisetum alopecuroides*, is easily one of the most popular and easy-to-grow ornamental grasses. Their tuft-like fountains of narrow foliage, in addition to their stunning plumage, make nice airy statements in the garden.

Many species of ferns **(BOTTOM)** are presented at the Morris Arboretum's Fernery. Ferns are a very ancient family of plants: early fern fossils predate the beginning of the Mesozoic era, 360 million years ago. They are older than land animals and far older than the dinosaurs. They were thriving on earth for 200 million years before the flowering plants evolved.

The colorful landscape at Morris **(PAGES 40-41)** includes Eastern Redbud, *Cercis Canadensis*; Korean Azalea, *Rhododendron yedoense*, Flowering Dogwood, *Cornus florida*, and Waite Redbud, *Cercis Canadensis 'Alba'*.

Flowering Dogwood **(BELOW)**, *Cornus florida f. rubra*, is a year-round flowering tree. It blooms in late spring, and has white, red, or pink blooms. In the summer it will grow red fruit known as rose hips. This popular plant has been known by many names, including false boxwood, cornelian tree, Florida dogwood, spindle tree, bird cherry, and nature's mistake.

Purple Robe **(LEFT)**, *Nierembergia*, has neat, spreading mounds of fine-textured foliage smothered with blue-violet flowers all summer long.

Daffodil **(FOREGROUND, LEFT, BOTTOM)**, *Nacissus*, is a narcissus with a trumpet that is as long or longer than the surrounding petals. Wild daffodils caused the first wildlife protection legislation in England. The flowers were so popular in the Stuart court that the peasants and gypsies would go into the fields and pick them by the thousands to sell at the court.

Saucer Magnolia **(BACKGROUND, LEFT, BOTTOM)**, *Magnolia soulangiana*, is a good specimen tree because of its attractive pink flowers.

Fragrant Viburnum **(BELOW, RIGHT)** *Viburnum burkwoodii*, has spring flowers that resemble hydrangea. The plant is often called snowball viburnum because of the large lower clusters that are pink in bud, turning to white in bloom.

Historic Fallsington

Places like Williamsburg, Virginia, and Sturbridge Village, Massachusetts, have buildings that were brought together to form a tourist attraction or at least are in an area that has been set aside for controlled access. Fallsington, Bucks County, is still the real thing—a functioning town with a variety of architectural styles dating from a log cabin of the 1680s to Victorian elegance from two centuries later.

There is no entrance gate and no entrance fee (although there is a fee for a guided tour of three buildings: the Moon-Williamson log house, the Burgess-Lippincott house, and the Stagecoach Tavern). Visitors can simply park, get a map at the headquarters of Historic Fallsington, Inc., and wander around to their heart's content.

Many of the homes have attractive gardens (which need to be admired from the street since the homes are privately owned and occupied) and that's what makes it a point of interest for those touring Philadelphia area gardens.

It is said that no other village in the region possesses such a concentration of old, remarkably untouched buildings on their original sites. The first settlers were English Quakers who arrived five years before William Penn. In 1690 they started worshipping in the new meetinghouse they had built, and Penn worshipped with them there when he returned from London.

Most of the early information about the village and its residents comes from minutes of the Meetings for Business held by Falls Monthly Meeting of the Religious Society of Friends. The meetinghouse was used as a point of reference in most of the early road surveys, and was the nucleus around which the village developed.

By 1728 the first meetinghouse was too small and a new one was built nearby, with the old building given over to use as a schoolhouse. In 1768 the established landowners pursued real estate development in a conscious effort to foster growth of a town; this was the first year in which "Fallsington" was used on deeds.

After a long, cold winter, Historic Fallsington is a good place to visit on a warm spring day when the dogwood and other spring bushes are in full flower.

In the 1820s, new houses **(RIGHT)** went up in Fallsington in the Federal style on the five roads that radiate out from the town square.

The Hough House **(BELOW)** is a handsome stone building of the 18th century facing Meeting House Square. In the back stand the ruins of the tannery owned by John Merrick.

Stagecoach Tavern **(RIGHT)** was built before 1798, when a liquor license was granted to operate it as a tavern. The building belonged to John McCormick, a well-to-do cordwainer. The building was a hotel, a circus venue, and a hardware store before it was restored in1960 by Historic Fallsington, Inc.

Historic Fallsington **(FAR RIGHT)** grew up around a 1690 Quaker meetinghouse that was frequented by William Penn, who lived nearby at Pennsbury Manor.

In 1789 a still larger meetinghouse was built. By 1798 the number of travelers and farmers going to the ferries and wharves of the nearby Delaware River called for a tavern. A general store flourished. All these buildings plus the houses of the tanner, the carpenter, the tailor, and the saddler still exist, circling the central Meetinghouse Square.

Visitors Information
Village streets open daily. Tours available for fee 10 a.m. to 4 p.m. Mondays to Saturdays, May to October, and 12 noon to 4 p.m. Sundays.

Historic Fallsington
4 Yardley Avenue • Fallsington, PA 19054
(215) 295-6567 • http://www.bucksnet.com/hisfalls

There are 2,000 species of plants that are native to "Penn's Woods," and nearly 1,000 of those species can be found throughout the 100 acres of Bowman's Hill Wildflower Preserve in Bucks County. This amazing collection includes more than 80 native species designated as Plants of Special Concern in Pennsylvania, including rare, endangered, and threatened plants.

The preserve started in a conversation between Mrs. Henry Parry, chairman of the Bucks County Federation of Women's Clubs, and W. Wilson Heinitsh, who was employed by the then Pennsylvania Department of Forests and Waters as a consultant for Washington Crossing Historic Park. The two met at that park and talked about the possibility of a sanctuary for Pennsylvania native plants with nature trails so visitors could appreciate the splendor of the state year-round.

The 100-acre Bowman's Hill Wildflower Preserve has nearly 1,000 species of native plants in a naturalistic setting of woodlands, meadows, a pond, and a creek. More than two dozen different trails covering about 2.5 miles are laid out to showcase the various plant species.

Wildflower Preserve

Support for their vision came from the Federation of Garden Clubs of Pennsylvania and the Council for the Preservation of Natural Beauty in Pennsylvania. That council made a gift to the Washington Crossing Park Commission that enabled it to set aside 100 acres in a portion of the park north of Bowman's Hill Tower as a living memorial to the patriots of George Washington's army who camped in the area during the Revolutionary War.

The Preserve's mission today is to lead people to a greater appreciation of native plants, to an understanding of their importance to all life, and to a commitment to the preservation of a healthy and diverse natural world. Unlike other botanical gardens, which tend to have plantings from many areas of the world, Bowman's Hill focuses exclusively on native plants.

To help promote its goal of educating the public, the Preserve offers a guided tour each day from mid-March to mid-October at 2 p.m. Planning your visit to take advantage of this tour will help you get the most from your visit. (The staff is very accommodating to people who arrive in the morning unaware of the tour time, suggesting that they walk around on their own, go off premises to have lunch, and then return for the tour.)

The property is crisscrossed by a series of short inter-connecting trails on either side of Pidcock Creek that visitors can walk. When you pay your admission fee, staff will suggest the trails that have the most interesting plants in bloom at the time you are there. The trail map lists blooming highlights for most months of the year and there also is a handout on native plants of various types that can be used to attract birds to your garden at home.

The Turk's Cap Lily **(BELOW LEFT)**, *Lilium superbum*, is among the largest members of the Lily family, reaching heights of nearly three feet. A single plant can produce up to 40 blooms.

The Wild Geranium **(BELOW RIGHT)**, *Geranium maculatum*, is a favorite in the wild garden due to its attractive foliage and flowers that require little or no maintenance.

Cinquefoil **(RIGHT)**, *Potentilla*, is rich in tannin and has been used in tanning for centuries. The plant was brought to European gardens from the Himalayas as early as the 1800s.

Obedient Plant **(FAR RIGHT, TOP)**, *Physostegia virginiana*, gets its common name because when the flowers are moved to the side, they remain in that position. Another name is False Dragonhead on account of the supposed resemblance to a European plant by that name.

Bee Balm **(RIGHT, BOTTOM LEFT)**, *Monarda didyma*, was brewed into tea by America's early colonists to protest the British tax on tea.

Blazing Star **(RIGHT, BOTTOM RIGHT)**, *Liatris scariosa*, looks excellent in a formal perennial garden or in larger groupings in a prairie meadow planting.

On my visit on a rare sunny day for the Spring of 2003, I followed several trails that led me to the small pond. There I encountered several men with serious camera gear, including very long telephoto lenses. I saw several turtles in the pond that were of interest to them but, until I asked what they were photographing, completely missed a snake lying in the water looking very much like the stick that was next to it.

Headquarters closed Mondays (except Monday holidays), Easter, Christmas, New Year's, Thanksgiving, and the day after Thanksgiving. Open Tuesday to Saturday 9 a.m. to 5 p.m. and Sunday 12 noon to 5 p.m. Trails open until dusk. Admission fee includes guided tour when offered.

Bowman's Hill Wildflower Preserve

1635 River Road (Pa. Rte. 32)• New Hope, PA 18939-0685
(215) 862-2924 • http://www.bhwp.org

Large-Flowered Trillium **(LEFT, TOP)**, *Trillium grandiflorum*, is called a "trillium" because the flower parts appear in threes, along with a whorl of three, broad, egg-shaped leaves.

Virginia Bluebell **(LEFT, BOTTOM LEFT)**, *Mertensia virginiana*, a member of the Boraginaceae Family, can be found in the northern two-thirds of the U.S. The genus is named for the German botanist Franz Karl Mertens (1764-1831).

Day Lily **(LEFT, BOTTOM RIGHT)** is not native to Pennsylvania *and often is seen as an invasive nuisance and removed from landscapes.*

Celandine Poppy **(RIGHT)**, *Stylophorum diphyllum*, blooms in April and May. Although generally native farther west than Pennsylvania, it still is commonly found here, probably as an escapee from cultivation.

(BELOW), a path of Blue Bells wind their way into the woods.

Delaware Valley College

Visiting the arboretum at the suburban Philadelphia campus of Delaware Valley College was a particular pleasure for us because we were able to take time to visit with Howard Eyre, a good friend who has been teaching at the college for several years.

The college was founded in 1896 as the National Farm School and the concept for a campus-wide arboretum dates back that far. National Farm School founder Joseph Krauskopf included an arboretum in his original plans for the school, but it wasn't until 70 years later, in 1966, that the arboretum was actually recognized and named.

The arboretum was named in honor of Henry Schmieder, a faculty member of the college from 1921 to 1964. He is remembered as a gifted teacher who had the ability to teach a wide variety of subjects in liberal arts, science, and agriculture. Schmieder was described by college president emeritus Joshua Feldstein as "a man with an intensely inquiring mind; a man who never ceased to be a student of the life he found everywhere about him."

At the time of his death, Schmieder was busily cataloging the arboretum collection and had plans for its expansion to make the campus a living resource for students, the community, and the horticulture industry.

The arboretum is intended to be a living laboratory, complementing and enhancing the work of the college's Department of Ornamental Horticulture and Environmental Design by emphasizing the combination of scholarship and applied experience.

Its primary mission is education through display of common and unusual plants in pleasing combinations and landscapes. It is used for teaching and research and provides lecture series, workshops, tours, children's programs, industry events, and involvement in community beautification and betterment.

Special collections of the Schmieder Arboretum include the gazebo annual and vine display garden; beech collection; magnolia collection; day lily/ornamental grass garden; Martin Brooks dwarf conifer collection; Lois Burpee herb garden; iris, peony, and poppy collection; woodland walk; and Herbst winter walk.

Students, staff, and visitors have an idyllic view **(LEFT)** in front of Lasker Hall on the Delaware Valley College campus.

Golden Yew **(ABOVE)**, *Taxus baccata Aurescens*, is native to Britain and particularly common in England and Wales, where they have been planted in many churchyards. These evergreen trees grow very slowly and live for many hundreds of years. Some old yew trees are believed to be over 2000 years old. Longbows were made from yew, and this durable wood has been used in turning wooden bowls and as a veneer by furniture makers.

Students dream of warm weather **(RIGHT)** as snow blankets the ground in front of Mandell Hall at Delaware Valley College.

Improvements underway include a redesign and re-landscaping of the college's North Gate, a comprehensive tree inventory and campus CAD mapping project, and a new training program for those who offer guided tours of the facility.

Visitor Information
The college grounds are open dawn to dusk daily; greenhouses are open only on weekdays. Free self-guided tours. There is a charge for guided tours by appointment.

Henry Schmieder Arboretum of Delaware Valley College
700 East Butler Avenue (U.S. 202) • Doylestown, PA 18901
(215) 489-2283 • http://www.delvalcol.edu

Highlands Mansion and Gardens

Once again we have a Quaker to thank for property that preserves nature near thriving communities. The Highlands is described as a charming secret garden hidden behind massive stone walls that beckons all who visit the 44-acre estate in Philadelphia's northwest suburbs.

Quaker lawyer Anthony Morris, who at one time was Speaker of the Pennsylvania House of Representatives, built The Highlands in 1796 as a summer house. Four different families have owned the site, where several early presidents of the United States were entertained. Each made significant additions to the mansion and gardens.

Chinese Wisteria, *Wisteria sinensis*, is a legume that is very popular as an ornamental a legume, that is very popular as an ornamental. Wisteria is known for the beauty of its long, cascading flowers. Japanese and Chinese wisteria are often used for bonsai, but American and Kentucky wisteria should also do well.

In 1917, Caroline Sinkler, an influential woman in Philadelphia society, purchased The Highlands as a country house and developed the two-acre formal garden that included a number of paths, each ending in a focal point of a sculpture or statuary.

Long herbaceous beds, a parterre, and a central fountain were notable features of her garden, which won a Pennsylvania Horticultural Society Gold Medal for Excellence in 1933. (A parterre is a garden on flat ground, in which the pattern of the garden is usually as important as the plants. Parterres are most often placed next to multistory buildings because the pattern of the garden is best appreciated from above.

Parterres reached their peak of development during the 17th Century, when the French garden was the most influential style in Europe, so the three styles of parterres are usually referred to by their French names.)

Tours of the mansion are available on a limited schedule, but the grounds are open daily for a walk back in time. In the parterre herb garden is an armillary sphere installed by Caroline Sinkler as the focal point for that area. I was particularly interested in it because we had just bought one at a craft show for our backyard in Harrisburg.

A massive stone archway **(LEFT)** frames a gardener at The Highlands.

Huge stone walls surround the gardens, which offer an unrivaled example of early 20th century estate gardening. Here, Trumpet Vine **(TOP)**, *Campsis radicans,* grows in front of the Fortress-like house.

Day Lily **(BOTTOM RIGHT)**, *Hemerocallis cultivar,* is one of the most popular garden perennials.

Bleeding Heart **(PAGES 62-63)**, Dicentra apectabilis, is a member of the poppy family. The strangely structured flowers give it its common name.

The armillary sphere is an ancient astronomical instrument. The arrow in it is to be aligned with the North Star and the metal rings or bands depict an antiquated theory of the rotation of the heavens around the earth.

Down a hill in front of the mansion is an octagonal springhouse built by Anthony Morris about 1800. George Sheaff, a later owner, used the springhouse to store and process dairy products. Containers of milk were placed in a stream on the lower level

Periwinkle **(RIGHT, TOP)**, *Vinca minor*, is a light woodland plant that is ideally used to form an evergreen ground cover under trees in a semi-shady position.

Bluet **(BELOW)**, *Houstonia caerulea*, is also known as Quaker Ladies, Innocence, and Little Washerwoman.

Flowering Dogwood **(RIGHT)**, *Cornus florida*, graces the front of the mansion at The Highlands.

Orris Root **(FAR RIGHT)**, *Iris pallida variegata*, is the dried and ground root of a Dalmatian iris. It is a fixative used in potpourri to enhance color and fragrance.

to keep the milk cool. In the 20th century, the springhouse was used as a dressing house for a swimming pool that was put in beyond the building.

Visitors Information
Open 9 a.m. to dusk daily. Guided mansion tours at 1:30 p.m. and 3 p.m., Mondays to Fridays. Fee for tour. Grounds free.

The Highlands Mansion and Gardens
7001 Sheaff Lane • Ft. Washington, PA 19034 • (215) 641-2687

Welkinweir

The Green Valleys Association was founded in 1964 by landowners in northern Chester County who were threatened by the proposed damming of French Creek. Originally established as the French Creek Watershed Association, the group expanded in 1972 to oversee all five of northern and eastern Chester County Schuylkill River watersheds—Pigeon Creek, Stony Creek, Pickering Creek, French Creek, and Valley Creek.

Welkinweir is the 162-acre headquarters and educational center of the Green Valleys Association. Everett Rodebaugh, Green Valleys Association founder, and his wife Grace, had purchased the property during the depression when it was a declining farm. They restored the land by reestablishing native trees and meadows. And a series of ponds was constructed in the valley. Acquisition of an entire nursery led to the beginning of formal planting around the house.

The Rodebaughs conveyed the property to the association in 1997 to ensure its continued use as a site for observing and learning from nature.

It has become a popular arboretum for its educational programs, walking trails, and the presence of five rare Franlinia trees (*Franklinia alatamaha*). While quiet and understated compared to some of the other sites on our tour, my visit there was quite pleasant and provided a much-needed respite from the traffic that clogged local roads as I made my way to Welkinweir. The fact that it's a little hard to find makes it all the more worthwhile once you are there.

Pick up a visitor guide and map from the information board that is near the parking lot. It points out that Welkinweir's hillside slopes overlook a secluded stream valley caught in a series of ponds, offering dramatic views of classic undisturbed Chester County. Ponds, wetlands, meadows, and woods provide a diversity of habitats to permit visitors observation of a range of birds and wildlife in their natural environment. The woodland trails allow for short or long hikes and also connect hikers with the Horseshoe Trail.

Seasonal interest in the gardens include spring blossoms of cherries, magnolias,

The pond at Welkinweir **(TOP)** is hidden from easy view in the summer among many green trees and shrubs.

Springtime brings flashes of color to the forest at Welkinweir **(LEFT),** such as the Japanese maple, *Acer palmatum 'Atropurpureum'*.

Trees clothed in their spring leaves **(PAGES 68-69)** rise above the ponds constructed in the stream valley.

dogwoods, daffodils, and Welkinweir's Azalea Lane. In the summer, perennials bloom in the barn ruins and white water lilies are reflected in the pond. Falls displays the foliage of native swamp and sugar maples, sweet gun, franklinia, and sourwood mixed with a variety of Japanese maples. And winter brings the quiet of resting plants, the interest of bark and structure, and the solitude of the Pinetum that was presented to the Rodebaughs by horticulturist Phillip Livingston.

I walked some of the trails in happy solitude and then came across two college-age students who were taking photographs. My time at Welkinweir left me in a pleasant and relaxed frame of mind as I headed to the Pennsylvania Turnpike and home.

Visitors Information
Hours of operation vary seasonally. Call for information. Suggested donation of $5 for grounds. House and garden tours for groups by appointment only.

Welkinweir
1368 Prize Road • Pughtown, PA 19465
(610) 469-7543 • http://www.greenvalleys.org/welkinweir.asp

Weeping Canadian Hemlock **(LEFT)**, *Tsuga Canadensis 'Pendula'*, is a widely known and used plant, staked and trained to develop height and character. It also is known as Sargent's Weeping Hemlock and has been described as "music in the form of a tree."

Everett and Grace Rodenbaugh, who purchased the property that would become Welkinweir during the Depression and transformed it into an estate and sanctuary for biodiversity **(BELOW)**, acquired a local nursery to supply the formal gardens around the house.

The Springhouse sits in the meadow **(RIGHT)**, next to a Flowering Dogwood, *Cornus florida.*

Jenkins Arboretum

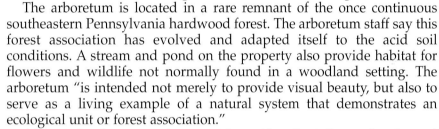

Located just a few blocks off U.S. Route 30—Philadelphia's Main Line—is a jewel of a small arboretum that preserves beauty and peace in the midst of the hurly burly of an incredibly busy world.

The arboretum first occupied 20 acres that had been the property of H. Lawrence and Elisabeth Phillippe Jenkins. As a living memorial to his wife, who had been an avid gardener and wildlife enthusiast, Jenkins established the Elisabeth Phillippe Jenkins Foundation and the Jenkins Arboretum. He directed in his will that the property should become a "public park, arboretum, and wildlife sanctuary for the use of the public and responsible organizations engaged in the study of arboriculture, horticulture, and wildlife for educational and scientific purposes...."

In 1971, Mrs. Louisa P. Browning, owner of an adjoining property, donated her 26 acres to the arboretum, more than doubling its size to its current configuration.

The arboretum is located in a rare remnant of the once continuous southeastern Pennsylvania hardwood forest. The arboretum staff say this forest association has evolved and adapted itself to the acid soil conditions. A stream and pond on the property also provide habitat for flowers and wildlife not normally found in a woodland setting. The arboretum "is intended not merely to provide visual beauty, but also to serve as a living example of a natural system that demonstrates an ecological unit or forest association."

After study of many environmental considerations, those who planned the arboretum made a decision to develop it with an emphasis on azaleas and rhododendrons and other related plants suited to the woodland conditions of the site. There also are many interesting and colorful wildflowers, many of which are perennials. Many different types of ferns offer a variety of textures and shades of green.

There is a Discovery Guide available that indexes many of the arboretum's marked trees and provides interesting notes about them. Ask for it at the administration building before starting your walk. The Guide does not follow a set trail or path, rather allowing you to wander the grounds at will, looking for trees containing a brown diamond-shaped marker with a T followed by a number. That's the identification that can be looked up in the Guide to read the "story of the tree."

As the Guide says, "the arboretum is a community of plants and each plant has its own unique story. We would like to acquaint you with some of the trees and share their stories with you. It's not intended that you complete this Guide in one visit, or even in two or three visits. Rather, we hope you come back often and learn something new each time."

Tulip Tree **(LEFT)**, *Liriodendron tulipifera*, is the state tree of Indiana, Kentucky, and Tennessee. It also is known as yellow poplar, tulip poplar, white poplar, and whitewood. A large tree, it is the tallest of the eastern hardwoods. It grows rapidly and is an important timber and shade tree. The wood is valuable for veneer and many other uses. Songbirds and game birds, rabbits, squirrels and mice feed on the seeds. Whitetail deer browse the young growth.

Rhododendron **(ABOVE)**, *Rhododendron 'Mary Fleming'*, is a small-leaved rhododendron that is low-growing and spreading. It is covered with numerous pale yellow flowers that have blotches and streaks of salmon. Rhododendrons are ancient plants, with fossils dating back to the Miocene era.

(PAGES 74 AND 75) Pink flowers at top left are on a Japanese Flowering Cherry, *Prunus serrulata "kwanzan'*, while below that is Shadbush or Serviceberry, *Amelanchier sp.*

One tree whose story cannot be told at the arboretum is the Pennsylvania State Tree, the Canadian hemlock. In the eastern United States these trees are being attacked by the hemlock woolly adelgid, a parasitic insect that literally sucks the life juices from the trees. Because of damage to its hemlocks, the arboretum has had to fell all of them. Botanists are experimenting with imported Japanese and Chinese ladybugs that naturally feed on the adelgids, along with an adelgid-killing fungus. Only time will tell if remaining hemlocks in the east will be able to withstand the adelgid's onslaught.

In the spring of 2003, which seemed to have many more cloudy and rainy days than sunny, I managed to catch a break and visit Jenkins on a warm, sunny day under a beautiful blue sky. The day was so nice for walking around and the property so pleasant that I wished for a larger Jenkins. There are several walks and trails laid out from the administration building, but it literally can take just a few minutes to stroll from one end of the property to the other. The plantings are spectacular along the way,

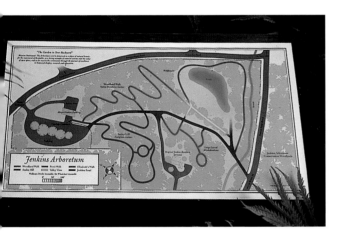

Forest Sunflower **(LEFT)**, *Helianthus decapetalus*, is also known as the thin-leaved sunflower. It is identified by its thin, rough leaves and is commonly found at the edge of wooded areas and thickets in moist areas from July to August.

Jenkins Arboretum has a number of trails **(ABOVE)** visitors can walk to see various parts of the property.

Wild Bergamot **(RIGHT)**, *Monarda fistulosa*, is often found in meadows with sandy soil and dry conditions. This aromatic herbaceous perennial can be made as a tea and inhaled to sooth bronchial complaints and ease colds. Thymol contained in the plant has been used as a stimulant and to relieve digestive flatulence and nausea.

with a particularly colorful section along what it known as Jenkins Road on the way to the pond.

While auto traffic on busy Devon State Road sometimes can be seen and heard, Jenkins Arboretum provides a much-needed oasis in the busy Philadelphia suburbs.

Yarrow **(ABOVE)**, *Achillea millefolium*, contains chemicals that help the blood to clot and reportedly was given by Achilles, the hero of Homer's Iliad, to his soldiers to help staunch the flow of blood from their wounds during the Trojan War.

Garden Phlox **(RIGHT)**, *Phlox paniculata*, comes in many colors and often is used as a major feature of summer gardens. The word "phlox" comes from the Greek word for "flame," and was given this plant because many of its blossoms are red.

Jenkins Arboretum
631 Berwyn Baptist Road • Devon, PA 19333
(610) 647-8870 • http://www.jenkinsarboretum.org

Chanticleer

Never has there been a more apt marketing tagline than the description of Chanticleer as "a pleasure garden." Not available as a jogging venue, not particularly interested in educating people about botany, Chanticleer exists to bring visitors pleasure in sights, sounds, and smells that are not soon forgotten. It is small—only 31 acres—but extraordinarily successful in its mission.

Named for a castle in England in a story by William Thackeray, the story of Pennsylvania's Chanticleer starts with Adolph Rosengarten, Sr., head of Rosengarten and Sons chemical company. In 1912 he bought seven acres of land and built a large house on it for his family. Over succeeding years, his son, Adolph, Jr., expanded the acreage and consolidated the holdings into a 31-acre estate. There are two large houses on the property, the main house and the house now used as the administration building that was built for Adolph, Jr'.s sister Emily. A third home, which had been occupied by Adolph, Jr., and his family, was pulled down in 1999 and a stunning ruin was built on the foundation.

Now managed by a non-profit foundation, Chanticleer has been designed as a pleasure garden to illustrate the beauty of the art of horticulture. Thousands of bulbs bloom in spring, followed by orchards of flowering trees with native wildflowers blooming in the woods. A vegetable garden complements a cut-flower garden. Courtyards are a framework for unusual combinations of herbaceous perennials, punctuated by pots of tropical plants.

On a beautiful spring day, Chanticleer sparkles as one looks out on a Sweet Cherry **(LEFT)**, *Prunus avium*, underplanted with Narcissus 'Ice Follies', which was developed more than 50 years ago in Noordwijk, a small Dutch coastal town nestled in the windswept dunes that hold off the waters of the North Sea. A favorite in this rugged setting, 'Ice Follies' has proved to be one of the all-time great naturalizers around the globe.

One of the showiest and longest-lasting tulips is known as Sport of Monte Carlo **(ABOVE)**, *Tulipa monsella*, with its canary yellow petals with blood red flames and streaks in the middle of each petaloid.

Chanticleer's tennis court **(NEXT PAGE)** has been transformed into a dynamic garden, originally designed to showcase herbaceous plants for summer and fall.

Visitors receive a simple map for a self-guided walk through the garden. Few of the plants are labeled, as if those in charge don't want us to have to think about the plants and learn their scientific names. Rather, there are benches throughout the garden to encourage visitors to stop and absorb the pleasures it offers. And there are dramatic uses of water throughout so that we hear the tranquil sound of water running or dripping almost everywhere we go.

The Chanticleer mansion house **(FAR LEFT)** was built by chemical company president Adolph Rosengarten, Sr. His family started with seven acres in 1912 and over the years expanded and consolidated the holdings into a 31-acre estate.

Ornamental Onion **(LEFT)**, *Allium sphaerocephalon*, also is known as drumsticks.

Wide walking paths **(BELOW)** take visitors through the "edgy" elements of the "pleasure garden."

This hardy water lily **(BOTTOM)**, *Nymphaea 'James Brydon'*, shows off its color next to a Variegated Figwort, *Serophularia suriculata 'variegata'*.

85

Textures **(ABOVE)** abound in the pleasure garden of Chanticleer.

Water plays a key role at Chanticleer **(RIGHT, TOP)**, including Bell's Run and a large pond.

Sorrel Tree **(RIGHT)**, *Oxydendron arborea*, is a tree that no one notices until something happens. In mid-summer, when other trees' flowers have long been forgotten, sorrel bears clusters of white flowers like lily of the valley. Each flower is an exquisite white bell. Sorrel is fragrant, and a source of good honey.

Visitors Information
Open 10 a.m. to 5 p.m. Wednesday to Saturday, April to October. Open until 8 p.m. on Fridays in May, June, July, and August. Admission fee. Guided group tours Wednesday, Thursday, and Friday by reservation.

Chanticleer
786 Church Road • Wayne, PA 19087
(610) 687-4163 • http://www.chanticleergarden.org

Despite its unpleasant-sounding name, Giant Hogweed **(BELOW, LEFT)**, *Heracleum mantegazzianum*, creates a pretty pattern as the sun shines through it.

False Spirea **(BELOW)**, *Astilbe arendsii*, Astilbe 'Deutschland' arendsii, is most noted for its fluffy flower spikes that bloom in pink and white from late spring to early summer. The fragrant flowers attract butterflies and make nice dried flowers.

A ruin garden **(RIGHT)** was built in 1999 on the site where Adolph Rosengarten, Jr., lived most of his life in Minder House. After the house was razed, construction of the ruin garden began. Originally the plan was to use the partially dismantled house as the ruin, but for safety reasons the only part left of the original house is the foundation.

Bryn Mawr College Arboretum

My first visit to the Bryn Mawr campus was on a December day several years ago when I accompanied other senior executives from The Hospital Association of Pennsylvania, where I was vice president for communications, to attend a health care summit featuring President Bill Clinton. At the time, my niece, Jessica, was a student there.

My main memories of the campus then are of snipers on top of some of the buildings and the Secret Service unwrapping and clumsily re-wrapping Christmas presents I had brought for Jessie. (Back then, I naively didn't see a problem in bringing the presents. Sadly, I know better now.)

My latest visit was much different, coming on a wonderfully sunny spring day and accompanied by Jessie's father, my brother Warren.

We wandered around some of the buildings and then entered through the gate to the main quadrangle where students were in intense knots of conversation or sunning themselves.

One of Bryn Mawr's gifts to the United States (in addition to its many successful alumnae) is the "Collegiate Gothic" style of campus architecture. The Philadelphia architectural firm of Cope & Stewardson first developed the style for Bryn Mawr residence halls in the late 1800s. Later, architect Louis Kahn earned accolades for his innovative design of Erdman Hall as a core of common living spaces surrounded by a continuous lattice of individual bedrooms.

Weeping Higan Cherry **(LEFT)**, *Prunus subhirtella 'Pendula'*, has drooping bare branches that are said to lend a grace to the landscape even in winter. In spring, there is nothing quite like a weeping higan cherry in full bloom. It should be located at a site where it will attract attention, since its form is attractive year-round.

Bryn Mawr College makes good use of Weeping Higan Cherry **(ABOVE)** along walkways and framing buildings.

91

The campus is a fascinating study in contrasts between the Collegiate Gothic structures and those that are much more strikingly modern in design.

Original landscaping of the campus was by Frederick Law Olmsted and Calvert Vaux, the designers of New York's Central Park. During the second half of the 19th century, Olmsted was one of the leading proponents of what came to be known as the City Beautiful movement in the United States. He was the leading landscape architect of the post-Civil War generation and has been acknowledged as the founder of American landscape architecture.

Weeping Canadian Hemlock **(ABOVE)**, *Tsuga Canadensis 'Pendula'*, is considered one of the most beautiful conifers. Pendula is a weeping, graceful cultivar that works well in a border or as a lawn specimen. It shouldn't be hidden behind anything taller. Here it sets off the turreted gray stone of a college building.

Landscaping plays an important role on the Bryn Mawr College campus **(RIGHT)** in accenting the varying building styles and designs.

Bryn Mawr College is listed on the National Register of Historic Places and its M. Carey Thomas Library is a National Historic Landmark.

The arboretum actually is the entire 135-acre English landscape-style campus of shrubs, massive trees, and spectacular vistas. Unlike some of the other colleges included on our tour, Bryn Mawr does not offer specific information or self-guided tours of its garden holdings, preferring to allow people to appreciate them in context of the buildings and other aspects of campus life.

Visitors Information
Open daily. Free admission.

Bryn Mawr College Arboretum
101 N. Merion Avenue • Bryn Mawr, PA 19010
(610) 526-5000 • http://www.brynmawr.edu

The Bryn Mawr visitor friendly campus has benches for resting and **(BELOW)** unusual plantings. Blue Star, *amsonia hubrechtii* blooms in late spring and has golden yellow foliage in the fall.

American College Arboretum

Founded in 1927, The American College is the nation's oldest and largest academically accredited educational institution devoted exclusively to financial services. Located on a 35-acre campus in Bryn Mawr, the college serves more than 35,000 students, predominantly through distance education. The American College offers an array of specialized designation programs, a Master of Science degree in financial services, and customized continuing education programs for those pursuing a career in financial services.

The college originally was located on the campus of the University of Pennsylvania in Philadelphia. Even in that urban setting, the college maintained a small but well-cared for garden. In 1961, it relocated to its current campus location in Bryn Mawr. The land for the new campus was the site of several large estates and was graced with a variety of many fine old trees. The existing landscape provided the college with an opportunity to expand and enhance its commitment to horticulture — a tradition that it proudly continues today.

As a public arboretum, the college's campus is valued and appreciated by numerous local residents who enjoy the walking paths among the plantings throughout the year. In addition to a variety of older trees, the campus forms a backdrop for a wooded stream valley, the Bette and Tom Wolff Ponds, and developing garden areas. The arboretum continues to grow and dedicated tree programs have added to the diversity of the species available to the public.

The ongoing growth of the arboretum has been carefully orchestrated as part of a master plan designed by renowned architects Aldo Giurgola and Ehrman Mitchell, perhaps best known for their design of the Liberty Bell Pavilion in Philadelphia's Independent National Historical Park. The design of the site and the manner in which the buildings have been integrated into the landscape have resulted in a visually cohesive experience for campus visitors. The architects placed campus buildings along the crests of hills, enclosing the stream valley, gardens, and laws, providing the

Daffodil **(LEFT)**, *Narcissus casseta*, gets its scientific name from the Greek god Narcissus, who looked into a pool, saw his reflection, and fell in love with himself. The name daffodil is commonly given to all narcissus with large trumpets. Wild daffodils caused the first wildlife protective legislation in England.

property with a sense of internal space while allowing nature to flow through the center of the campus.

American College officials say the institution has always maintained that an environment of excellence in horticulture, architecture, and art inspires excellence in its educational programs. Designation of the campus as an arboretum by the college's board of trustees in 1994 was an affirmation of that philosophy.

My brother Warren and I visited on a beautiful sunny afternoon as people from the surrounding community came over to eat lunch outside or bring children for a day in the park.

A walking tour is available on the College's Web site. Among the sites on the tour are a fragrance garden in the courtyard of the Gregg Conference Center, an herb wall, and a pedestrian walking path that leads visitors through the conifer collection with an overlook. Other highlights of the walking tour include views of Wolff Ponds, the stream valley, Goodwin Daffodil Hill, the cottage garden at McCahan Hall, the Boettner woodland

Giant Dogwood **(RIGHT)** *Cornus controversa*, has a horizontal, wide-spreading branch pattern and creates a lovely display in late spring with a profusion of white flowers.

Daffodil **(BELOW)**, *Narcissus las vegas*, has white and yellow flowers that are said to be the best-performing out of all of the bicolor varieties.

Daffodil **(BELOW, RIGHT)**, *Narcissus tahiti*, is a spectacular show-stopper and award winner. The double rose-like blooms earned it Daffodil of the Year honors in 1999.

Sugar Maple **(FAR RIGHT)**, *Acer saccharum*, is considered one of the most beautiful trees in the world.

garden, a native Franklinia tree first seen by John Bartram in Georgia and not seen in the wild since 1803, and the Theodore J. Shalack memorial garden.

I was particularly taken by the Bette and Tom Wolff Ponds with their ducks and Japanese coy, as well as the picnic area tucked away in the beauty. A plaque at Wolff ponds describes them as "two ponds connected by a bridge of mutual understanding and respect, by our deep love for each other, our family, and God. They are dedicated to our business and this institution. Relax here and enjoy the peace and solace of these surroundings."

Visitor Information
Open daily dawn to dusk. Free admission. Group tours by appointment.

American College Arboretum
270 S. Bryn Mawr Avenue • Bryn Mawr, PA 19010
(610) 526-1229 • http://www.amercoll.edu/About_Us/arboretum.asp

Haverford College

In the late 17th century, Welsh Quakers settled on 40,000 acres of land ceded to them by William Penn, intending to establish a barony. The effort failed, however, and the so-called Welsh Tract was divided. Then, in 1831, a distinguished group of New York and Philadelphia Quakers purchased 198.5 acres of land in the center of the tract and two years later opened Haverford College. English gardener William Carvill was brought here to convert the farmland into a functioning college campus. His design reflected the influence of Sir Humphrey Repton, one of England's great landscape architects. (Carvill also is credited with bringing rugby, Haverford College's oldest sport, to the campus.)

At the beginning of the 1900s, a concerned group recognized the need to preserve the college's rich heritage and formed the Campus Club. The group functioned for more than 50 years, much of that time under the leadership of Edward Woolman of the Class of 1893.

Although the Campus Club was established in 1901, it was not until 1928 that the idea of a "comprehensive planting of trees" at Haverford was recorded in the group's minutes. In response to that idea, superintendent of grounds Robert J. Johnston developed a plan for a scientific collection of trees to be arranged in generic and family groupings, and a planting site was selected near the southwestern boundary of the

The Haverford College arboretum is a favorite place for local residents to walk their dogs and observe Canada geese and other wildlife.

college. This ultimately became the Ryan Pinetum as over a 20-year period members of the Campus Club transplanted hundreds of young conifers from their nursery to the site.

In time, however, interest waned due to the loss of many Campus Club members. In the early 1970s, John A. Silver, a graduate of the Class of 1925, envisioned an organization that would carry on the work of the Campus Club. Through his efforts, the Campus Arboretum Association was founded in 1974 with a commitment to continue the tradition and heritage of campus beautification at Haverford College.

Interest in the Pinetum was rekindled in 1988, and an application was submitted to the Institute of Museum Services, a federal agency that offers project support to the nation's museums, and the project was completed in 1990. Named for Dick and Nancy Ryan, whose long-term efforts led to restoration of the site, the Pinetum today is recognized as one of the finest in an area with many outstanding collections and provides a unique educational resource for conifer study in a setting of exceptional beauty.

Although Haverford's arboretum is clearly one of the finest and most extensive on the tour, it is not as visitor friendly as one would like. Campus maps show the arboretum headquarters as part of the physical plant building, making it somewhat hard to locate. A helpful student directed my brother and me to the Campus Center,

but the information desk wasn't staffed and the campus maps there were difficult to follow.

We started walking somewhat aimlessly and came upon the arboretum building quite by accident. Fortunately, a staff member was just leaving the area and was very helpful in directing us to the nearby Pinetum and pointing us in the direction of the Zen garden outside the dining hall, a significant hike from the arboretum building.

There are two very attractive brochures at the arboretum building—one on the arboretum itself and one on the Pinetum. But they both deal only with trees and don't make any reference to the plantings around the campus or the Zen garden.

Trails and paths wind through the beautiful campus inviting visitors to spend time in rest and relaxation.

While I might wish for better signage and more information, that would only serve to make a wonderful location still better. I like this statement at the back of the arboretum brochure:

> As you conclude your tour of Haverford's special trees, we hope you will reflect upon the Reptonian landscape, interpreted by William Carvill in 1835, which is spread before you: rolling lawns, sweeping vistas, and placement of trees in artfully 'naturalistic' ways. For more than 150 years, stewards of Haverford's landscape have endeavored to preserve this rich heritage for the enjoyment of those who teach, study, and work on the Haverford campus and for those who visit this very special place.

Visitors Information
Open daily. Free admission.

Haverford College Arboretum
370 Lancaster Avenue • Haverford, PA 19041
(610) 896-1101 • http://www.haverford.edu/arboretum/home.htm

Walking the Haverford College campus in spring **(LEFT)** brings pleasure and the sense of calm and peace that was the intent of those who have designed and maintained this treasure.

Japanese Flowering Dogwood **(LEFT)**, *Cornus kousa*, is planted as a specimen, near a patio, or in groupings. It blooms later and with a softer petal flower than the white flowering dogwood.

Majestic Sycamore trees **(BELOW)**, *Platanus occidentalis*, tower over Haverford's campus buildings.

Paper Birch **(RIGHT, TOP)**, *Betula papyrifera*, is named for its paper-like bark. It is the most popular birch for ornamental use. The bark turns a bright white when the tree matures.

Bold Cypress **(RIGHT, BOTTOM)**, *Taxodium distichum*, has a trunk that tapers gradually from a wide, flaring base, giving it the form of the shoulder of a bottle.

Longwood Gardens

While by far the largest and most visitor-centered of the gardens on our tour, Longwood Gardens still has a friendly, welcoming, family-oriented feel to it.

In 1700, George Peirce acquired 402 acres west of Philadelphia in the Brandywine River Valley from William Penn. Peirce's descendants farmed the land and in 1798 began planting an arboretum that by 1850 was recognized as one of the finest in the nation.

Pierre S. du Pont bought the farm in 1906 to preserve the trees and, from 1907 until 1954, he personally designed most of what visitors enjoy today. Since then, according to Longwood Gardens' publicity materials, it has matured into a "magnificent horticultural showplace filled with countless opportunities for learning and enjoyment."

Toadflax **(LEFT FOREGROUND)**, *Linaria maroccanai*, also known as Spurred Snapdragon, is frequently neglected in gardens because it is not a showy plant. The flowers are fragile and thin and last only one day, but they appear in such profusions that plants give the appearance of being continuously in flower. In the background are tulips, *tulipa cv.*

Poinsettia **(RIGHT)**, *Euphorbia pulcherrima*, is one of the highlights of the Christmas display in the conservatory.

Today, Longwood Gardens covers 1,050 acres of gardens, woodlands, and meadows; 20 outdoor gardens; 20 indoor gardens within four acres of greenhouses; 11,000 different types of plants; illuminated fountains; extensive educational and research programs; and 800 events on the grounds each year.

The property hosts 900,000 visitors from around the world each year and even on the weekday spring morning when I visited, the garden walks were comfortably filled with people ranging from retired couples to suburban mothers with children in strollers to school classes.

There is so much to see and do that one should plan to spend several hours at Longwood, and to go during various seasons and for some of the special events that

Fittonia **(RIGHT)**, *Fittonia verschaffeltii*, is often called Nerve Plant due to the markings on the leaves. It is found in the tropical rain forest in Peru.

Chrysanthemum **(BELOW)**, *Chrysanethemum x morifolium 'Orange Bowl'*, is a hybrid developed from four species native to Asia.

The East Conservatory, part of this main conservatory building **(RIGHT)**, is undergoing renovations 2003 to fall of 2005, and will have Mediterranean and subtropical-climate flora and large-scale displays of blooming plants thriving year round surrounded by a dynamic setting of courtyards, fountains, and pools.

Queen Victoria Agave **(BELOW LEFT)**, *Agave victoriae-reginae*, is a native of Mexico, but was named for the British Queen Victoria.

Pennsylvania Amish visitors look over the lily pond **(BELOW RIGHT)** at Longwood Gardens.

107

are held each year. If geography makes it appropriate, consider a Frequent Visitor pass—it has paid for itself once you go more than four times in a year.

The day that I was there most recently, I was eager to start at the Flower Garden Walk to see the riot of color from 90,000 spring bulbs that had been planted at the end of last year. I wasn't disappointed, but also was interested to see that members of a class of elementary-age children were busy taking lots of pictures—of a butterscotch and white cat that was happily sunbathing among the colored tulips.

Chrysanthemum **(BELOW)**, *Chrysanthemum*, has many classifications, including these anemone mums grown in the Longwood Conservatory.

Another form of chrysanthemum is the spider mum **(RIGHT)**. This is a 'Yellow Knight'.

After Mother's Day, the Flower Garden Walk is completely replanted with summer annuals, perennials, and foliage plants.

As the sometimes harried owner of Tucker, an 18-month-old border collie dog, who could run and play 24 hours a day, I was interested in a sign indicating that Longwood uses border collies to herd the Canada geese that have set up residence on the grounds. Visitors are asked to respect the dogs' abilities to persuade the geese to move their nests, but not to interfere with their work. The geese, according to the sign, are

Visitors strolling through Longwood's outdoor gardens **(RIGHT)** often come across beds of bright, contrasting colors that make interesting patterns.

Zinnia **(FAR RIGHT),** Zinnia *'Profusion Orange'*, is a Gold Medal winner because of its disease resistance. It is easy to grow and provides considerable color throughout the season.

This Double Early Tulip **(PAGES 112-113)** is *Tulipa 'Monte Carlo'*. Its butter yellow petals are very fragrant. The wide-open double flowers of Double Earlies resemble peonies.

110

"bothered but not harmed" by the attention from the dogs. I wished I had seen one or more of them in action, and left wondering if they could use one more with boundless energy and a need to work.

Visitors often are so busy admiring flowers, plants, bushes, and trees that they overlook the grass on which they sometimes walk. But the staff at Longwood recognizes that the lawn is the most challenging thing they grow. For the last five years,

they have been dealing with it organically, not using any pesticides or other poisons, despite the fact that they say the lawn gets every disease imaginable. They use a golf course mix to achieve the beautiful green backdrop that sets off all the other plantings.

In the Conservatory, the indoor gardens regularly evoke cries of "Isn't this beautiful." Marie Sipala, who often is at the counter distributing free audio tour sets that people can use to learn about the plants in the Conservatory, says it's not unusual for people to approach her as if she were responsible for all the beauty there. "People come to me and say 'This is beautiful'," she says, "and I just say 'thank you'."

The scope of what is accomplished at Longwood is brought out in an informative sign at one end of the Conservatory that indicates that where homeowners might

Rose Mallow **(FAR LEFT, TOP)**, *Hibiscus 'Lady Baltimore'*, has glowing neon pink blossoms with a satiny red center that earn it a special place in the garden.

Orchid **(TOP, RIGHT)**, *Orchid 'miltonia'*, looks like a giant pansy. They are beautifully patterned, often with pansy-like waterfall markings.

Bromeliad **(LEFT BOTTOM)**, *Neoregelia concentrica*, is among the most colorful of bromeliads. Most neos are from southeastern Brazil. Experts say the plant has been in cultivation since the middle of the 19th century. It grows naturally in cloud forests, and can reach two to three feet in diameter.

Wild Petunia **(BELOW)**, *Petunia integrifolia*, also is known as Petunia 'Pink Wave' and Petunia 'Purple Wave'.

Fancy Leafed Caladium **(LEFT)**, *Caladium candidum*, is a very showy foliage plant with bright red, pink, green and white variegated leaves that often are considered to be prettier than many flowers.

Rose of Sharon **(BELOW)**, *Hibiscus syriacus*, also is known as Shrub Althea. They add a lot of color, even through the heat of the summer.

Everlasting **(BELOW RIGHT)**, *Helichrysum fortaresii*, is in front of Spurflower, *Plectranthus*.

purchase a market pack with six plants to use in their landscape, Longwood needs hundreds and sometimes thousands to achieve the desired effect.

But Longwood isn't only about admiring beautiful plantings that we might not have in our home gardens. One part of the grounds is devoted to an Idea Garden, laid out to give home gardeners an idea of things they can do. There are separate beds in the Idea Garden for perennials, annuals, herbs, grasses, and shade-loving plants, all appropriate for southeastern Pennsylvania. Information sheets and growing tips also are available at the site.

In addition to all the steps taken to make Longwood appealing and useful to casual visitors, resources also have been devoted to scientific research, plant identification, and plant exploration. Most of the research effort goes into new crops, plant improvement, and cultural studies of plants grown for public display. Longwood also

has an extensive educational program that carries out du Pont's desire to establish "a school where students and others may receive instruction in the arts of horticulture and floriculture." For the past 30 years, as many as 5,000 students a year have participated in continuing education classes designed for both amateur and professional gardeners and nurseymen. Also, since 1958 some 1,000 students from all over the world have participated in one or more of seven intensive programs, ranging

Bengal Tiger Canna **(BELOW)**, *Canna 'Pretoria'*, has been described as "yelling tropical at the top of its lungs," but still is very hardy. Though some gardeners describe cannas as garish, others see these colorful, easy-to-grow plants as indispensable in the landscape. They are native to Central and South America, Malaysia, and Nepal.

Foxglove Excelsior **(RIGHT)**, *Digitalis purpurea 'Excelsior Mix'*, is a superior early bloomer with large spikes. Excelsior hybrids have flowers distributed all around the stem, rather than just on one side.

French Marigold **(FAR RIGHT)**, *Tagetes patula 'Queen Sophia'*, is native to Mexico. There are many forms and varieties of marigolds, with a considerable range of size and color. The plant was considered sacred by the Aztec Indians, who used them to decorate shrines and temples.

from internships to a two-year professional gardener training program to a master's degree program in public horticultural administration.

Longwood's year-round performing arts program is an outgrowth of du Pont's interest in music and theatre and takes advantage of the many performance spaces he created throughout the grounds and facilities. More than 400 events are held each year, ranging from organ and carillon concerts to outdoor folk and chamber music to Open Air Theatre productions with more than 100 people on stage before an audience of 1,500. Spectacular fireworks and fountain displays can attract 5,000 on a summer

Egyptian Starcluster **(LEFT)**, *Pentas lanceolata*, comes in red, white, lavender, purple, or shades of pink. Some are two-toned. All are extremely attractive to butterflies, and the red and dark pink varieties delight hummingbirds. Experts say it works well in butterfly beds and also is a wonderful annual when planted in drifts of uniform color.

Dwarf Peach **(BELOW)**, *Prunus persica 'Honey Babe'*, is a freestone peach. The peach is native to Asia, where its cultivation began around 800 BCE. The Chinese believe peaches impart long life. The peach came to southern Europe through Persia during the reign of Augustus, and notable cultivars were developed under the reign of Louis XIV, king of France.

121

evening, and more than 200,000 visitors pass through the gates at Christmas time to ooh and ahh over 400,000 outdoor lights.

Visitors Information
Outdoor gardens and Conservatory open daily at 9 a.m. and 10 a.m. respectively and close at 6 p.m. April to October and 5 p.m. November to March. Longwood remains open many evenings during summer and at Christmas. Admission fee.

Longwood Gardens
Route 1 • Kennett Square, PA 19348
(610) 388-1000 • http://www.longwoodgardens.org

Summer Snapdragon **(FAR LEFT)**, *Angelonia angustifolia*, blooms over a long period in the summer. Angelonia is native to Mexico and the West Indies, where it is a sub-shrub. In the U.S. it is grown as an annual. It is unusually heat tolerant and requires almost no care.

Glory Bush **(LEFT, ABOVE)**, *Tibouchina grandifolia*, has been described as "one of nature's grand plants." Characterized by large, velvet leaves, in autumn the shrub is covered with white-centered purple flowers.

White sagebrush **(LEFT, BOTTOM, IN FOREGROUND)**, *Artemisia absinthium*, has soft gray foliage that makes it a good plant for toning down brighter colored flowers.

Purpletop Verbena **(LEFT, BOTTOM, IN BACKGROUND)**, *Verbena bonariensis*, is native to Brazil and Argentina. Gardening experts say the airy, see-through habit of purpletop verbena makes it a good choice for the front or middle of a mixed border.

Golden Candles **(BELOW)**, *Pachystachys lutea*, also is known as golden shrimp plant or lollipop plant.

Brandywine River Museum

Faced in the mid-1960s with the potential for significant industrial development in floodplain areas of Chester County's historic Brandywine Valley and the adverse impact such development would have on the water supply for several communities, a group of residents bought endangered land at auction and founded the Brandywine Conservancy in 1967.

In 1971, the Conservancy opened the Brandywine River Museum in Hoffman's Mill, a former gristmill on the banks of the Brandywine River. Now, more than four million visitors later, the museum has established an international reputation for its collection of works by three generations of the Wyeth family—N.C., Andrew, and Jamie—and its collection of American illustration, still life, and landscape painting.

In addition, the Conservancy's Environmental Management Center preserves the natural and cultural resources of the area and has been instrumental in permanently protecting more than 32,000 acres of land.

Seen through the window **(LEFT)** is a Silver Maple, *Acer saccharinum*.

This Downy Serviceberry, *Amelanchier x grandiflora*, **(RIGHT)**, is along the museum side of the driveway between the museum and the conservancy.

Wildflowers native to the Brandywine Valley bring color around the museum from spring through autumn. There also is a one-mile trail along the river that, the day I visited, was popular with an art class from a local senior high school whose members were busy sketching a variety of scenes while enjoying the warmth of the sun. Though short, the trail offers access to an alluvial forest, a mill dam, a power line right-of-way, a wetland area with boardwalk for visitors passing through it, and a floodplain meadow.

Visitors Information

Museum open daily 9:30 a.m. to 4:30 p.m. except Christmas Day. Gardens open daily dawn to dusk. Admission fee for museum; gardens free.

Brandywine River Museum
Route 1 • Chadds Ford, PA 19317
(610) 388-2700 • http://www.brandywinemuseum.org

Oakleaf Hydrangea **(LEFT, TOP)**, *Hydrangea quercifolia*, has large, coarse leaves that resemble those of an oak tree. Hydrangea's capacity for changing the color of its flowers was first noted in 1796. At that time it was thought that the flowers took their color from objects nearby casting shade on them. In 1875 it was discovered that the flowers turn blue if the plants are watered with a solution of aluminum or by mixing iron filings with the soil. To obtain pink flowers, it is necessary to use a fertilizer containing a high percentage of phosphorous.

This Day Lily, *Hemerocallis fulva*, **(LEFT)**, is often found along roadsides and in cultivation.

Tyler Arboretum

One of the oldest and largest arboreta in the northeastern United States, Tyler Arboretum occupies 650 acres in central Delaware County. It began as a private collection of two brothers, Jacob and Minshall Painter. In 1681, William Penn had signed a lease and purchase agreement with Thomas Minshall, an English Quaker, for property in Pennsylvania that contained the site now occupied by the arboretum.

Between 1681 and 1944, the property was home to eight generations of the same Minshall/Painter/Tyler family. Jacob and Minshall Painter were fascinated by the popular 19th century study of natural history. During their lifetimes, they assembled large collections of dried plants, rocks, and other specimens.

In 1825, the Painters set aside some of their land to begin the systematic planting of more than 1,000 varieties of trees and shrubs. More than 20 of the original Painter

Forsythia, *Forsythia suspensa*, a fast-growing shrub, is known for bringing color to us in the late winter and early spring. Often its branches are cut and brought inside and forced as a means of brightening an otherwise dreary winter day.

trees still survive, including a giant sequoia that is the symbol of Tyler Arboretum.

In 1944, Laura Tyler, a direct descendant of Thomas Minshall, bequeathed the property to a board of trustees that had been established to direct and oversee the land as an arboretum.

Tyler sees itself as distinct from other area arboreta in that its mature plant collections are laid out in a natural setting. In addition to the historic Painter trees, several of which are state champions, Tyler has several other collections, including an 85-acre Pinetum with pines, spruces, hemlocks, firs, cedars, false cypresses, and larches; rhododendron, flowering cherry, crabapple, holly, magnolia, and lilac collections; a Native Woodland Walk, a fragrant garden, butterfly garden, and bird garden; Pink Hill, a barren of serpentine stone on which grows endemic wildflowers;

and 450 uncultivated acres that remain natural and contain 20 miles of marked trails well used by hikers, birders, and naturalists.

The centerpiece of the arboretum and the most lasting legacy of the Painter brothers is their botanic collection, which at times numbered more than 1,100 specimens. While continuing to manage their family's farming interests on the property that now contains Tyler, by the 1860s the Painters had essentially transformed a large portion of the estate into an arboretum.

Today, only 23 of the brothers' original plantings remain. But they did leave behind journals, letters, planting lists, and numerous scribbled notations that help today's visitors understand not only their reasons for planting, but what they were trying to achieve with their collections.

Beginning in 1995, Tyler staff began efforts to propagate several Painter trees, including the giant sequoia, swamp white oak, and white oak. Professionals are actively searching for ways to preserve Tyler's horticultural legacy with the hope of sharing the results with the broader horticultural community.

One could happily spend hours at Tyler and return on many occasions. Those who live close enough should certainly consider becoming members so they could visit as often as they wish without paying a daily entrance fee.

A well-prepared visitors guide includes a map showing the seven trails ranging in length from .9 mile (25 minutes) to 8.5 miles (4 hours). Trails are color coded with blazes to follow on trees throughout the trail system and are graded in walking difficulty from easy to moderate/steep. All trails circle back to a common trailhead and

Among the treats for the eye **(LEFT)** at Tyler are Lavender, *Lavendula angustifolia*, a Mediterranean shrub that is cultivated for its aromatic flowers in the U.S. and Europe. The name Lavender is derived from the Latin lavare, meaning "to wash," as it was added to baths for its therapeutic properties and delightful fragrance. Both the flowers and leaves have been used by different cultures for various health purposes. Also seen here are Yarrow, *Achillea 'Moonshine'*, and Green Lavender Cotton, *Santolina rosmarinifolia*.

Tyler Arboretum's educational signs **(ABOVE)** help visitors to understand the dynamics of various types of land and its use.

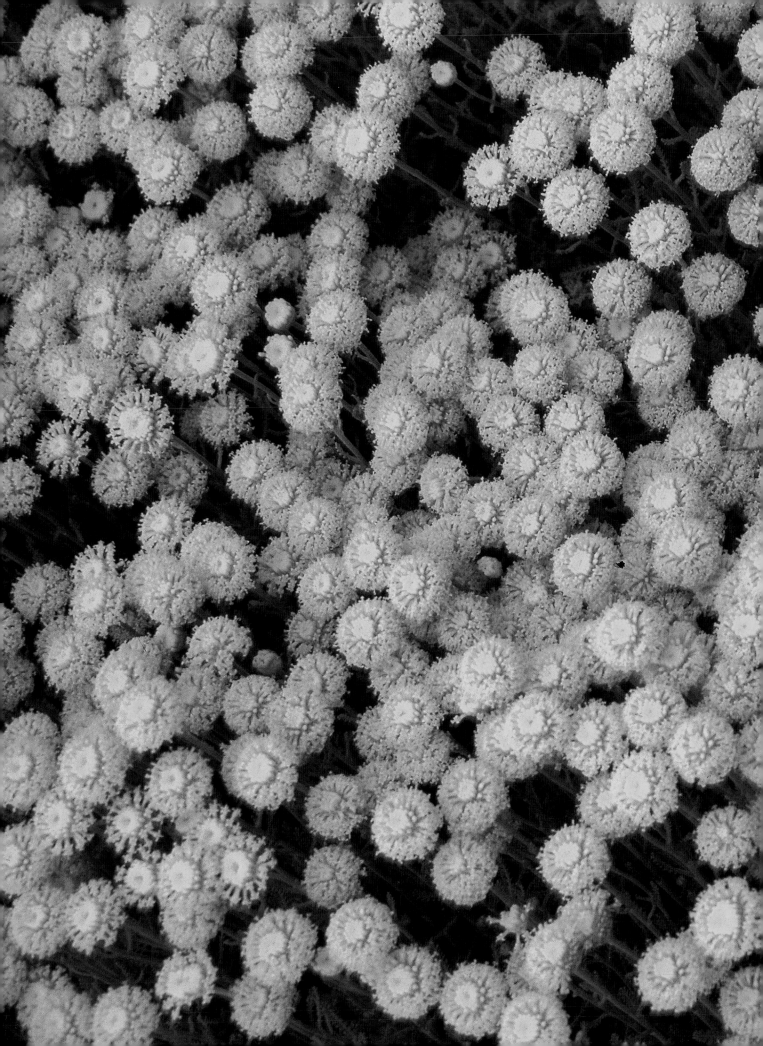

sometimes intersect so that you can cross from one trail to another if you choose.

Outside of the trail system are the various collections, the fragrant garden, butterfly river, raptor roost, meadow maze, Pinetum, and native woodland walk.

Also on the grounds are the Painter Library—built by the Painter brothers to house their collection of books, specimens, and scientific equipment, including their own printing press—and Lachford Hall, the house the Minshall, Painter, and Tyler families

Green Lavender Cotton **(PAGES 132-133)**, *Santolina rosmarinifolia*, has green leaves that are very aromatic. The green lavender cotton is used as low border or edging.

Garden Phlox **(LEFT, TOP)**, *Phlox paniculata 'Crème de Menthe'*, is a cultivar of garden phlox that is known primarily for its creamy-margined variegated foliage, rather than its inflorescences.

Japanese Pieris **(LEFT, BOTTOM)**, *Pieris japonica 'Variegata'*, has leaves with white margins that may be tinged with pink in spring. There are drooping white flowers, possibly less abundant than many other cultivars.

A butterfly **(BOTTOM, RIGHT)** visits Mountain Mint, *Pycnanthemum sp.*

Cedar of Lebanon **(RIGHT, TOP)**, *Cedrus libani*, was first found in Lebanon, but has spread to other areas of the world. The wood is decay resistant and it is never eaten by insect larvae. It is of a beautiful red tone, solid, and free from knots.

Evergreen ornamental grasses **(RIGHT, BOTTOM)**, such as *Festuca glanca 'Elijah Blue'*, add interest to gardens. This species is especially good because it retains its bright blue color through the summer.

134

occupied between 1738 and 1937. Today, half the building is an historic museum with the families' housewares and furniture, and half is the arboretum's administrative offices. Tours of the library and Lachford Hall are offered April to July and September through October.

Visitors Information
Open daily 9 a.m. to between 4 p.m. and 8 p.m. depending on the season. Admission fee.

Tyler Arboretum
515 Painter Road • Media, PA 19063
(610) 566-9134 • http://www.tylerarboretum.org

Scott Arboretum of Swarthmore College

While several of the Philadelphia-area colleges have arboreta, some formal areas and others essentially the entire campus, it is clear that Swarthmore College takes the presence of the Scott Arboretum very seriously. The college refers to it as a "garden of ideas and suggestions" that covers more than 300 acres of the campus and exhibits more than 4,000 kinds of ornamental plants, with an emphasis on the best trees, shrubs, vines, and perennials for use in the region's home gardens.

The arboretum is a memorial to Arthur Hoyt Scott, an amateur horticulturist of some renown who was the son of the founder of the Scott Paper Company and a member of the Swarthmore class of 1895. Through an initial bequest of $85,000 from his family, the arboretum was created in 1929 with a mission to display plants suited for home gardens and educate the public.

Swarthmore, one of the nation's leading independent liberal arts colleges, has a beautiful campus just outside of Philadelphia. The arboretum's collections and gardens are lovingly set on this busy campus. Plants are labeled with scientific and common names and grouped in collections to make easy and meaningful comparisons.

The arboretum also is responsible for management of Crum Woods, a tract of woods along Crum Creek at the back of the campus that is a vital green space in a highly developed area. Replanted in the 1930s, it is actively maintained as a native woodland.

On a perfect spring day just after graduation at the school, my border collie Tucker and I had a chance to walk some of the grounds. The arboretum staff has prepared a walking tour brochure that is available in a box outside the arboretum office at the corner of College Avenue and Cedar Lane, just a short walk from the designated parking area for visitors. The tour loops through much of the campus, starting with the Scott Entrance Garden at the arboretum building.

An Okame Flowering Cherry **(LEFT)**, *Prunus 'Okame'*, bends over a slab showing that Swarthmore College was founded in 1864. Purple Allium **(ABOVE)**, *Allium aflatunense*, graces the Swarthmore College campus.

A short walk brings visitors to the old Quaker meetinghouse on the campus (Swarthmore was founded by Quakers and retains many values of the Religious Society of Friends) and the nearby Meetinghouse Woods that, according to legend, are remnants of the forest that once covered the grounds.

There are collections of lilacs, hydrangeas, viburnum, magnolias, and rhododendrons, as well as several named gardens honoring graduates or administrators. Some gardens cater to a particular season of the year while others, such

There are many varieties of Japanese Flowering Cherry on the Swarthmore campus including Prunus *'Sekiyama'* **(LEFT)**, *Prunus x yedoensis* **(BELOW)**, *Prunus 'Ojochin'* **(RIGHT)**, and *Prunus incisa* **(FAR RIGHT)**. There are more than 100 species in the Prunus genus. They are often used in bonsai because they will survive and even bloom when artificially dwarfed and restricted to a small pot.

as the fragrance garden, bring together fragrant flowers, foliage, and bark. In the Pinetum is a collection of conifers, including most of the hardy kinds of cone-bearing trees.

The Biostream was designed as a creative way to handle storm water. A rock-filled drainage bed allows groundwater to recharge and helps to filter out pollutants. The drainage area is surrounded by a variety of flowering shrubs and perennials.

Back at the arboretum office, the Terry Shane Teaching Garden features an annual border that changes each season, an arbor, and a water garden.

Visitors Information
Grounds open year-round dawn to dusk. Free. Office hours 8:30 a.m. to 12 noon and 1 p.m. to 4:30 p.m. Mondays to Fridays, except closed Friday afternoons June to August and closed July 4, Thanksgiving, day after Thanksgiving, and December 25 to January 1.

Scott Arboretum of Swarthmore College
500 College Avenue • Swarthmore, PA 19081
(610) 328-8025 • http://www.scottarboretum.org

Rhododendron **(LEFT)**, *Rhododendron X*, is one of more than 1,000 species of rhody that exist today. The genus covers everything from shrubs a few inches tall to trees that are 100 feet tall. Rhododendrons are distributed over much of the world.

Flowering Plum **(RIGHT)**, *Prunus triloba 'Multiplex'*, puts out large, double pink flowers in April and May. It also is known as Flowering Almond. It is a native of China.

Japanese Maple **(BELOW)**, *Acer palmatum 'Dissectum'*, is one of a large number of diverse maple trees.

141

Index

Index